Dear Friend,

You're just the one we had in mind as we planned this new book. To begin with, we know there are lots of ways you use a cookbook. You read it—simply because you like to read about food. Or you use it to "look up a recipe." You use a cookbook to learn to cook—or as a refresher course, to become a better, more up-to-the-minute cook.

We kept you in mind when we tested and tasted each recipe, and when we asked our home testers to tell us how the recipes fit into their lives. We know you're busy, so we've used convenience foods and shortcuts wherever we could. We know you demand quality, so every recipe is our taste-tempting best.

In short, we've given you a cookbook to cook with, to be comfortable with. We hope it will become a friendly member of your kitchen family, that it will answer your questions, help solve your problems and make the eating and living in your house just a little easier, a lot more fun.

Betty Crocker

Betty Crocker's
DINNER FOR TWO

Director of Photography: JOHN GARETTI

BANTAM BOOKS
TORONTO · NEW YORK · LONDON · SYDNEY

*This low-priced Bantam Book
has been completely reset in a type face
designed for easy reading, and was printed
from new plates. It contains the complete
text of the original hard-cover edition.*
NOT ONE WORD HAS BEEN OMITTED.

BETTY CROCKER'S DINNER FOR TWO

*A Bantam Book / published by arrangement with
Western Publishing Company, Inc.*

PRINTING HISTORY

Golden Press edition published March 1973

Bantam edition / February 1975

2nd printing .... January 1975	7th printing ...... June 1977
3rd printing .... May 1975	8th printing ...... June 1977
4th printing ...... August 1975	9th printing .... January 1978
5th printing .... June 1976	10th printing .. September 1978
6th printing ..... January 1977	11th printing ..... March 1980
12th printing ... October 1981	

ISBN   0-553-20656-7

Published simultaneously in the United States and Canada

*Bantam Books are published by Bantam Books, Inc. Its trademark,
consisting of the words "Bantam Books" and the portrayal of a
rooster, is Registered in U.S. Patent and Trademark Office and in
other countries. Marca Registrada. Bantam Books, Inc., 666 Fifth
Avenue, New York, New York 10103.*

PRINTED IN THE UNITED STATES OF AMERICA

21   20   19   18   17   16   15   14   13   12

CONTENTS

WHAT'S SO SPECIAL
ABOUT COOKING FOR TWO?

Two is a very good number. Or so the songwriters say. The joys of being a twosome have been catalogued in enough lyrics to reach the moon (in June) and back again. But somehow, very few of the choruses praise the pleasures of cooking for two.

Could it be because it's considered more of a problem than a pleasure? If so, this book will surely help dispel that notion. Not that the shopping, planning and preparation involved are all fun and games. But there are some very definite advantages to setting two places (or even one) which you may not have given much thought to before.

Cheer for Your Choices

The advantages of cooking for few ... what are they? "Choice" is the word that almost says it all. Think about it a bit. When you cook small, you're more apt to allow yourself the out-of-season fruit or out-of-reach meat—a choice you'd never consider if you were cooking for more. And you can take full advantage of the wealth of frozen, prepared and packaged foods that are especially geared to ones and twos.

Then there's the matter of mood. More choices! Pairs or singles needn't be confined to same-place dining. If you don't feel like setting your every-night table, go where the spirit moves you. You can "tray" it in the living room for a TV special, play it cool outdoors on a stuffy night or be casual as you please at the kitchen counter.

Plotting the Plan

The twosome does have special problems, it's true. But chin up—this book will show you how to tackle them.

To begin with, there's the matter of marketing. A major dither for anyone, but particularly so for doubles or singles. But all the recipes in this book are just the right size, so you'll know exactly how much to buy. To take you one step further, the bulk of the "Basic Know-How" chapter is devoted to helping you shop wisely. You'll find solutions for other problem posers, too. There are complete meal plans for rush times, for tight-money times, for urge-to-splurge times. All just for two. But that doesn't mean you have to think small. The "Planning Ahead" chapter actually encourages you to think big—to take advantage of the economies and pleasures of family-size roasts and the variety that can come from their leftovers.

What's more, every single recipe and every menu has been tested in the Betty Crocker Kitchens and by two-somes all across the country. So we know they'll work for you.

Once you've tried these menus "by the book," feel free to improvise—to put new lyrics to the music. Switch vegetables, swap salads, ring in a different entrée. For a heartier meal, add rolls or biscuits; for a lighter one, ease up on dessert. And many "bonus" main dishes have been included in each chapter to menu-mix as you please.

The Balancing Act

So you make your menu by putting your favorites together, right? Not quite. Good nutrition counts, too. And heavily. The menus in the book were planned with an eye to nutritional balance, so you're bound to pick up a tip or two. And you can do the same on your own by keeping the "Basic Four" guidelines in mind.

But remember dinner is only one of your meals. You need to be clued in as to what else is (or was) on the eating program for the rest of the day to do the planning job properly. Dinner can plug in some of the gaps, but it shouldn't be expected to carry more than a third of the daily load.

THE "BASIC FOUR"
You Need These Every Day

1. Meats

2 or more servings (also includes poultry, fish, eggs, dried beans or peas and peanut butter)

2. Vegetables and Fruits

4 or more servings (plan on one dark green or yellow vegetable every other day and one citrus fruit daily)

3. Milk

2 or more cups (also includes cheese and ice cream)

4. Breads and Cereals

4 or more servings (whole grain, enriched, restored or fortified)

Remember to include sweets, fats and extra servings from the basic four groups to help round out meals and provide additional food energy and food values.

Contrast Is the Key

Anything else? Just a few more ground rules—and they can be summed up in a simple phrase: Think contrast.

Think contrast in color. A white fish with a bright vegetable, a pale slaw with a ring of green pepper, chocolate pudding with a jolt of snowy topping. When you plan the kinds of foods you serve, try to imagine how they'll look on the plate.

Think contrast in texture. Put something soft with something crisp. Pair something chewy with something smooth.

Think contrast in flavor. Spice is nice, but cool it with something mild. All bland makes a dull meal, and all tart isn't smart. Rarely would you care to repeat one food in the same meal, such as Waldorf salad and apple pie (even if apples *are* the best buy of the week).

Think contrast in temperature. Sultry day or not, one hot dish gives a meal more appeal. By the same token, an ice-cream dessert refreshes even on a frosty night.

Think contrast in shapes and sizes. This one is relatively easy. An example: If you're serving hamburger patties, carrots and potatoes, cut the carrots into sticks instead of rounds, and perhaps serve French fried or au gratin potatoes instead of little potato balls.

How's Your Timing?

Let's assume you've decided on a menu that rates an A in nutrition and appeal. What happens next makes the difference between calm and chaos. Scheduling enters the scene. Look over the timing hints given with many of the menus—particularly, and quite naturally, in the chapter called "When Minutes Matter." You'll realize that successful timing is more than a matter of instinct and luck. It's part common sense, part experience and part plain confidence. Common sense tells you, for instance, that you're plotting a collision course if everything requires last-minute attention. Basically, the more you can fix ahead (the night before, morning before or even an hour before), the easier it will be as "curtain time" approaches.

To avoid the pitfalls of sorry scheduling, jot down all the foods you plan to serve, then note the time you estimate it will take you to prepare and cook each one. Obviously, you'll start with the longest and work your way to the speediest. It's that simple.

Rely on cook-and-serve ware and any labor-saving appliances you may have to help speed things along. And if someone shares the just-before-you-serve jobs, you really have it made.

Flair—The Extra Dimension

You don't need an extensive (or expensive) wardrobe of linens, dishes and accessories to add flair to your table. Not at all. Chances are you already have everything it takes to add a special touch right at your fingertips. Simple things like a basket heaped with glossy lemons and limes, seashells piled in a wooden bowl, a small green plant, a coffee mug filled with daisies. Inexpensive place mats and napkins serve a practical purpose and add zing to your table.

And don't forget decorative garnishes . . . those unexpected little flicks of color and flavor that add an exclamation point to an everyday plate. Parsley was born to be the universal trim, but don't stop there. Try a sprig of mint, a few celery leaves or a pickle slice. Such simple ways to "style up" a dish.

Flair is letting the "creative you" be free to find beauty and surprise all around.

Now, read on. Use the ideas and recipes that follow as your starting point. Then add your own special touches, play up your own preferences. Discover the continuing adventure and reward in every "dinner for two" you share. Whether you are recently wed, apartment-sharers or a career couple . . . whether you are back to two . . . whether you are alone and on your own . . . you'll find that this book is the one for you.

WHEN MINUTES MATTER

**Easy dinners that let you shortcut—
without being shortchanged**

Steak Stroganoff
Parsleyed Noodles
Buttered Asparagus Spears
Herbed Tomatoes
Individual Brownie Alaskas

STEAK STROGANOFF

1 medium onion, thinly sliced
1 tablespoon salad oil
2 beef cubed steaks
2 tablespoons flour
2 tablespoons salad oil
½ teaspoon salt
¼ cup dairy sour cream
1 can (2 ounces) mushroom stems and pieces

In 8-inch skillet, cook and stir onion in 1 tablespoon oil until tender, about 4 minutes. Remove from skillet and set aside.

Coat steaks with flour. Heat 2 tablespoons oil in same skillet; cook steaks over medium heat, about 4 minutes on each side. Sprinkle with salt. Place steaks on warm platter or dinner plates.

Drain fat from skillet. Add onion, sour cream and mushrooms (with liquid) to skillet; heat, stirring occasionally. Serve sauce on steaks. *2 servings.*

PARSLEYED NOODLES

Cook 4 ounces noodles (about 1½ cups) in 1 quart boiling salted water (2 teaspoons salt) until tender, about 7 minutes. Drain noodles and return to saucepan. Add 1 tablespoon butter or margarine and 1 teaspoon parsley flakes and toss. *2 servings.*

HERBED TOMATOES

   1 medium or 2 small tomatoes, cut into slices
     Crisp salad greens
   2 tablespoons oil-and-vinegar dressing
     Salt and pepper
   ¼ teaspoon freeze-dried chives
     Dash thyme

Arrange tomato slices on salad greens. Drizzle dressing on tomatoes. Sprinkle with salt, pepper, chives and thyme. *2 servings.*

INDIVIDUAL BROWNIE ALASKAS

   2 Brownies (page 80), 3x3 inches, date bars or
     commercially prepared sponge shortcakes
     Vanilla, coffee or peppermint ice cream
   1 egg white
   2 tablespoons sugar

Place Brownies on ungreased baking sheet. Top each with scoop or slice of ice cream; place in freezer while preparing meringue. (Ice cream must be very hard before covering with meringue.)

Heat oven to 450°. Beat egg white until foamy. Beat in sugar gradually; continue beating until stiff and glossy. Do not underbeat. Quickly spread meringue on ice cream *and sides of brownies,* being careful to seal meringue to baking sheet. Bake until light brown, about 3 minutes. Place in freezer (up to 24 hours) or serve immediately. *2 servings.*

Tacos
Refried Beans
Fruit with Quick Custard Sauce

TACOS

½ pound ground beef
1 can (8 ounces) tomato sauce
2 tablespoons instant minced onion
½ teaspoon garlic salt
¼ teaspoon chili powder
  Dash pepper
4 or 5 taco shells
½ to ¾ cup shredded lettuce
½ cup shredded natural Cheddar cheese
½ cup chopped tomato, if desired
  Hot Sauce (below) or bottled taco sauce

In 8-inch skillet, cook and stir meat until brown. Drain off fat. Stir in tomato sauce, onion, garlic salt, chili powder and pepper. Simmer uncovered 15 minutes.

While meat mixture simmers, heat taco shells as directed on package. Fill taco shells with meat mixture. Top each with lettuce, cheese and chopped tomato. Serve with Hot Sauce. *4 or 5 tacos.*

Hot Sauce

Mix ⅓ cup chili sauce and ¼ teaspoon red pepper sauce or 1 teaspoon minced hot chili pepper.

Note: Shredded Swiss or mozzarella cheese can be substituted for the Cheddar cheese. And for variety, when filling the taco shells, add one of the following: ¼ cup chopped avocado, ¼ cup chopped olives, ¼ cup chopped onion or ¼ cup chopped green pepper.

FRUIT WITH QUICK CUSTARD SAUCE

1 **orange, pared and sectioned, or 1 can (11 ounces)
   mandarin orange segments, drained**
1 **banana**
¼ **cup canned vanilla pudding**
2 **tablespoons milk**

Divide orange sections between dessert dishes. Slice
banana into dishes. Mix pudding and milk; spoon onto
fruits. *2 servings*.

Variations

Pineapple with Quick Custard Sauce: Substitute 1 can
(13½ ounces) pineapple chunks, drained and chilled,
for the orange and banana. Top each serving with ½
teaspoon strawberry jelly.

Berries with Quick Custard Sauce: Substitute 1 cup
strawberry halves, raspberries or blueberries for the
orange and banana.

SOMETHING TO KNOW ABOUT...

Cut off the peel and white
membrane of the orange. Then
cut along both sides of each
dividing membrane until you
reach the core and can lift
out the orange section.

Dilled Salmon and Peas
Toasted English Muffins
Cherry Tomatoes
Mixed Fruits Supreme

DILLED SALMON AND PEAS

1 package (8 ounces) frozen green peas with cream
  sauce
1 can (8 ounces) salmon, drained
3 pitted ripe olives, sliced
½ teaspoon dill weed
½ teaspoon salt
1 tablespoon lemon juice
  English muffins, split and toasted

Cook peas as directed on package. Separate salmon
into pieces, removing skin and bone. Stir salmon, olives,
dill weed, salt and lemon juice into peas. Heat to boiling, stirring occasionally. Reduce heat; cover and simmer until salmon is hot, about 5 minutes. Serve on
muffins. *2 servings.*

MIXED FRUITS SUPREME

1 can (16 ounces) fruits for salad, drained
¼ cup dairy sour cream
¼ teaspoon almond extract
1½ teaspoons sugar
  Flaked coconut

Divide fruits between two 1-cup ovenproof dishes or
10-ounce custard cups. Mix sour cream, almond extract
and sugar; spoon on fruits. Sprinkle with coconut.

Set oven control at broil and/or 550°. Broil desserts
with tops about 3 inches from heat until coconut is
toasted, about 2 minutes. *2 servings.*

> **Quick Cheese Fondue**
> **Crisp Green Salad**
> **Fresh Fruit**

QUICK CHEESE FONDUE

- 1 can (10¾ ounces) condensed Cheddar cheese soup
- 1 cup shredded Cheddar, Swiss or Parmesan cheese (about 4 ounces)
- 2 green onions, finely chopped
- ⅛ teaspoon garlic powder
  Dash red pepper sauce
  Dippers (below)

In fondue pot, saucepan or chafing dish, heat soup and cheese over medium heat, stirring occasionally, until cheese is melted. Stir in onion, garlic powder and red pepper sauce. Serve with three or more of the Dippers, cut into bite-size pieces if necessary. If fondue becomes too thick, stir in small amount apple juice, white wine or beer. *2 servings.*

Dippers

Croutons
French bread
White or rye hard rolls
Toast sticks
Cooked asparagus
  (crisp-tender)
Cooked broccoli
  (crisp-tender)
Cooked Brussels sprouts
  (crisp-tender)
Cauliflower

Dried beef rolls
Cooked chicken or turkey
Frankfurters
Cooked ham
Luncheon meat
Cooked shrimp
Celery
Stuffed olives
Green onions
Green peppers
Cherry tomatoes

Baked Chicken with Sherry-Mushroom Sauce
Buttered Peas
Wild and White Rice
Spiced Peaches
Quick Orange Muffins
Coffee à la Mode

BAKED CHICKEN WITH SHERRY-MUSHROOM SAUCE

1 **pound ready-to-serve chicken pieces (4 or 5) or**
1 ready-to-serve chicken, split into halves
1 **can (10½ ounces) condensed cream of chicken soup**
1 **can (2 ounces) mushroom stems and pieces**
¼ **cup dry sherry or water**
¼ **to ½ teaspoon tarragon leaves**
⅛ **teaspoon garlic powder**
½ **teaspoon Worcestershire sauce**

Heat oven to 400°. Place chicken in ungreased baking pan, 9x9x2 inches. Mix soup, mushrooms (with liquid) and remaining ingredients; pour over chicken. Bake until chicken is hot and sauce is bubbly, about 20 minutes. *2 servings*.

Note: You can substitute 1 pickage (about 16 ounces) frozen fully cooked battered chicken halves for the ready-to-serve chicken. Bake chicken as directed on package except—after baking 25 minutes, pour soup mixture over chicken; bake 20 minutes.

BUTTERED PEAS

Heat oven to 400°. Place ½ package (10-ounce size) frozen green peas on piece of heavy-duty aluminum foil. Sprinkle ¼ teaspoon salt on peas; dot with 1 tablespoon butter or margarine. Wrap securely in foil. Bake until peas are tender, about 20 minutes. *2 servings*.

WILD AND WHITE RICE

½ **package (6-ounce size) seasoned long grain and**
  wild rice*
¾ **cup boiling water**
 1 **teaspoon butter or margarine**

Heat oven to 400°. Place rice in ungreased 2½-cup casserole; sprinkle seasoning mix on rice. Stir in water and add butter. Cover tightly and bake until rice is tender and water is absorbed, about 20 minutes. Stir rice before serving. *2 servings.*

* To use half the package, measure contents and divide in half (approximately ½ cup rice and 1 tablespoon plus 1½ teaspoons seasoning mix).

QUICK ORANGE MUFFINS

Measure 1 package (14 ounces) orange muffin mix; divide in half (approximately 1½ cups).* Prepare muffins as directed except—use half the mix, 1 egg and 3 tablespoons milk. *6 muffins.*

* To store remaining mix, close package securely; use within 3 weeks to make hot muffins for breakfast or brunch. Or if you prefer, make entire package and freeze leftover muffins to use as needed.

COFFEE À LA MODE

For each serving, pour hot strong coffee into coffee mugs to about ¾ full. Add scoop of vanilla or coffee ice cream and serve immediately.

Shrimp Boil
Hot Potato Salad
Warm French Bread
Brandied Peach Melba

SHRIMP BOIL

- 2 bottles or cans (12 ounces each) beer or 1 quart water
- 1 tablespoon salt
- ⅛ teaspoon instant minced garlic, if desired
- 1 pound fresh or frozen raw medium shrimp (in shells)
  Cocktail Sauce (below)
  Lemon Butter (below)

In large saucepan, heat beer, salt and garlic to boiling. Add shrimp; heat just to boiling. Reduce heat; cover and simmer until shrimp are pink, 3 to 5 minutes. Drain; serve shrimp with sauces. Each person peels his own shrimp—so be sure to provide a container for the discarded shells. *2 servings.*

Cocktail Sauce

- ¼ cup catsup
- 1 tablespoon horseradish
- 1 tablespoon lemon juice

Mix all ingredients. *⅓ cup.*

Lemon Butter

- ½ cup butter or margarine
- 1 tablespoon lemon juice
- 1 tablespoon snipped parsley
- ¼ teaspoon red pepper sauce

Heat all ingredients over low heat, stirring constantly, until butter is melted. Keep warm. *About ½ cup.*

HOT POTATO SALAD

 ½ **package (5.5-ounce size) scalloped potatoes***
1½ **cups water**
 1 **tablespoon wine vinegar**
 ¼ **cup sliced green onion**
 1 **teaspoon prepared mustard**
 2 **lettuce cups**
   Bacon-flavored vegetable protein chips

Place potato slices in 8-inch skillet; sprinkle sauce mix
on slices. Stir in water. Heat to boiling, stirring occasionally. Reduce heat; cover and simmer, stirring occasionally, until potatoes are tender, about 25 minutes.
Stir in vinegar, onion and mustard; cook until hot and
bubbly.

Spoon into lettuce cups; sprinkle with vegetable protein chips. Add a colorful garnish of green pepper
rings. *2 servings.*

* To use half the package, measure contents and divide
in half (approximately 1 cup potato slices and 3 tablespoons sauce mix).

To store remaining mix, close package securely; use
within 2 weeks to make Scalloped Potatoes with Ham
(page 155) or Quick Scalloped Potatoes (page 116).

BRANDIED PEACH MELBA

 4 **brandied peaches**
 ¼ **cup raspberry jelly**
   Vanilla ice cream

Place 2 peaches in each dessert dish. Melt jelly; pour
on peaches. Chill several hours. Top each serving with
ice cream. *2 servings.*

Note: Fresh or canned peach halves can be substituted
for the brandied peaches.

Smoked Pork Chops
Mashed Potatoes
Parsley-buttered Carrots
Sauerkraut Salad or Apple Slaw
Frosty Sherbet Sandwiches

SMOKED PORK CHOPS

Diagonally slash outer edge of fat on four ½-inch-thick smoked pork chops at 1-inch intervals to prevent curling. Set oven control at broil and/or 550°. Broil chops with tops 3 to 5 inches from heat until done, about 6 minutes on each side. *2 servings*.

Note: To panfry, rub 8-inch skillet with fat cut from chops. Cook chops over medium heat until done, about 3 minutes on each side.

PARSLEY-BUTTERED CARROTS

1 can (16 ounces) whole small carrots
1 tablespoon butter or margarine
1 teaspoon parsley flakes

Heat carrots (with liquid); drain. Dot with butter. Sprinkle with parsley flakes and toss. *2 servings*.

Note: Use the vegetable cooking liquid in soups, gravies and sauces whenever possible, as it contains vitamins and minerals.

SAUERKRAUT SALAD

1 can (8 ounces) sauerkraut, rinsed and well drained
¼ cup chopped green pepper
1 tablespoon chopped red onion
1 tablespoon sugar
¼ teaspoon caraway seed
¼ teaspoon salt
Dash pepper
2 tablespoons oil-and-vinegar dressing
Crisp salad greens

Toss all ingredients except salad greens in bowl. Cover and refrigerate at least 30 minutes. Drain. Serve on salad greens. *2 servings.*

Time-savers: Substitute 1 tablespoon dried mixed salad onions for the red onion and 1 teaspoon dried green bell pepper for the fresh pepper.

APPLE SLAW

1 pint coleslaw (from delicatessen)
1 red apple, chopped
Crumbled blue cheese

Mix coleslaw and apple in bowl; garnish with cheese. *2 servings.*

FROSTY SHERBET SANDWICHES

1 can (8 ounces) sliced pineapple, drained
Orange sherbet or vanilla ice cream
Apricot preserves
Diced roasted almonds

Place 1 pineapple slice on each dessert plate; top each with a scoop of sherbet. Cut 1 side of each remaining pineapple slice; twist and place on sherbet. Drizzle preserves on each serving; sprinkle with almonds. *2 servings.*

> **Herbed Lamb Chops**
> **Quick au Gratin Potatoes**
> **Broiled Zucchini**
> **Broiled Tomatoes**
> **Hard Rye Rolls**
> **Pears au Chocolat**

HERBED LAMB CHOPS

2 to 4 lamb rib, loin or shoulder chops, ¾ to 1 inch thick
¼ teaspoon oregano, rosemary or marjoram
Salt and pepper

Set oven control at broil and/or 550°. Diagonally slash outer edge of fat on chops at 1-inch intervals to prevent curling. Sprinkle oregano on chops. Place chops on rack in broiler pan. Broil with tops about 3 inches from heat until brown, about 6 minutes on each side. Season with salt and pepper. (Season after browning—salt tends to draw moisture to surface and delays browning.) Garnish with mint jelly. *2 servings.*

QUICK AU GRATIN POTATOES

Measure contents of 1 package (5.5 ounces) au gratin potatoes; divide in half (approximately 1 cup potato slices and 3 tablespoons sauce mix).* Place half the potato slices in 1-quart saucepan; sprinkle 3 tablespoons sauce mix on potato slices. Stir in half the amounts of butter, water and milk called for on package. Heat to boiling, stirring occasionally. Reduce heat; cover and simmer until potatoes are tender, about 20 minutes. *2 servings.*

* To store remaining mix, close package securely; use within 2 weeks. Prepare Quick au Gratin Potatoes again

and serve with ham, frankfurters, meatballs or hamburgers. Or use the remaining ½ package in Hamburger au Gratin Skillet (page 134) or Canadian Cheese Soup (page 84).

BROILED ZUCCHINI

Set oven control at broil and/or 550°. Remove stem and blossom ends from 2 medium zucchini. Cut each zucchini lengthwise in half.

Place cut sides down on rack in broiler pan. Broil about 3 inches from heat 6 minutes. Turn zucchini and brush each cut side with melted butter or margarine; season with salt and pepper. Broil until tender, about 6 minutes longer. *2 servings.*

BROILED TOMATOES

Set oven control at broil and/or 550°. Remove stem end from 1 medium tomato; cut tomato in half. Dot each half with ½ teaspoon butter or margarine; sprinkle with garlic salt, lemon pepper, and if desired, basil leaves, oregano leaves or savory. Broil tomato halves cut sides up with tops about 3 inches from heat until golden brown, about 5 minutes. *2 servings.*

PEARS AU CHOCOLAT

 1 **can (8 ounces) pear halves, drained**
⅛ **teaspoon peppermint extract**
½ **can (18-ounce size) chocolate pudding (1 cup)**

Place 2 pear halves in each dessert dish. Stir peppermint extract into pudding; spoon on pears. Garnish with dollop of whipped topping and maraschino cherry or mint leaf. *2 servings.*

Broiled Ham and Sweet Potatoes
Brussels Sprouts with Cashews
Lettuce Wedges with Tangy Corn Dressing
Banana Fondue Fritters

BROILED HAM AND SWEET POTATOES

1 fully cooked smoked ham slice, about ½ inch thick
1 can (8 ounces) sweet potatoes in syrup, drained
2 canned pineapple slices, well drained*
2 tablespoons orange marmalade

Set oven control at broil and/or 550°. Diagonally slash outer edge of fat on ham slice at 1-inch intervals to prevent curling. Place ham slice on rack in broiler pan. Broil ham slice with top 3 inches from heat until light brown, about 5 minutes.

Turn ham; place potatoes and pineapple on rack. Brush marmalade on potatoes and pineapple. Broil until potatoes and pineapple are hot and ham is light brown, about 5 minutes. *2 servings.*

* Extra pineapple slices? Top with cottage cheese for a salad or use in Pineapple Burgers (page 34).

BRUSSELS SPROUTS WITH CASHEWS

Cook 1 package (10 ounces) frozen Brussels sprouts as directed. Drain and return to saucepan. Add 2 tablespoons cashews, walnuts or sliced water chestnuts and 1 tablespoon butter or margarine; heat through. *2 servings.*

LETTUCE WEDGES WITH TANGY CORN DRESSING

Mix 2 tablespoons oil-and-vinegar dressing and ¼ cup corn relish.* Spoon on lettuce wedges.

* Extra corn relish? Serve later in the week as a zesty accompaniment for roast pork, veal, ham or chicken.

BANANA FONDUE FRITTERS

1 cup buttermilk baking mix
½ cup water
1 egg
¼ teaspoon almond extract
  Salad oil
2 bananas, cut into ½-inch slices
  Confectioners' sugar

Beat baking mix, water, egg and extract with rotary beater until smooth.

Pour oil into metal fondue pot to depth of 1 to 1½ inches. Heat on fondue stand over burner or on range to 375° or until 1-inch bread cube browns in 1 minute.

With long-handled fork, each person dips banana slice into batter, cooks it in hot oil until puffed and golden brown, then rolls fritter in confectioners' sugar. *2 generous servings.*

Variations

Apple Fondue Fritters: Substitute 2 apples, pared and cut into ½-inch slices, for the bananas. Roll fritters in cinnamon-sugar mixture instead of in confectioners' sugar.

Strawberry Fondue Fritters: Substitute ½ pint fresh strawberries for the bananas.

Pineapple Fondue Fritters: Substitute 1 can (13½ ounces) pineapple chunks, drained, for the bananas.

Minute Steaks with Butter Sauce
Mashed Potatoes
Chili Mixed Vegetables
Stuffed Pear Salad
Cake Parfaits or Spanish Sundaes

MINUTE STEAKS WITH BUTTER SAUCE

- 1 tablespoon salad oil
- 2 beef cubed steaks
  Garlic salt
- 2 tablespoons butter or margarine
- 1 teaspoon lemon juice
- 1 teaspoon Worcestershire sauce
- ½ teaspoon freeze-dried chives
- ¼ teaspoon dry mustard

Heat oil in 8-inch skillet; cook steaks over medium-high heat until brown, about 4 minutes on each side. Season with garlic salt. Remove steaks from skillet and keep warm.

Drain off fat. Melt butter in same skillet. Stir in remaining ingredients and heat. Place steaks on dinner plates; pour butter mixture on each. *2 servings.*

CHILI MIXED VEGETABLES

Cook ½ package (10-ounce size) frozen mixed vegetables* as directed except—use only half the amounts of water and salt called for on package. Drain. Add 1 tablespoon butter or margarine and ¼ teaspoon chili powder and toss. *2 servings.*

* Leftover frozen vegetables? Use in Shepherds' Pie (page 144). Or cook the entire package; season half as directed above and marinate the other half with salad dressing to serve as a salad the next day.

STUFFED PEAR SALAD

Drain 1 can (8 ounces) pear halves. Arrange on crisp salad greens. Fill centers of pear halves with cranberry sauce or relish, raspberry or strawberry jelly, fruit-flavored gelatin cubes or peanut butter. *2 servings*.

CAKE PARFAITS

Cut pound cake (from freezer), leftover Quick Date Cake (page 58) or fig bars into cubes. Layer cubes alternately in parfait glasses with one of the following:

Apricot or pineapple yogurt.
Orange sherbet.
Vanilla ice cream and chocolate sauce.
Whipped topping and grated orange peel.

SPANISH SUNDAES

Divide ½ can (18-ounce size) vanilla pudding (1 cup) between dessert dishes. Drizzle chocolate syrup or sauce on each and top with Spanish peanuts. *2 servings*.

Chicken Livers with Mushrooms
Toast Points
Green Beans
Tomato-Grapefruit Salad
Butterscotch Cake Sundaes or Nesselrode Sundaes

CHICKEN LIVERS WITH MUSHROOMS

½ pound fresh or frozen chicken livers
2 tablespoons butter or margarine
1 can (2 ounces) mushroom stems and pieces
¼ cup water
1 tablespoon flour
¼ teaspoon salt
⅛ teaspoon pepper
1 teaspoon parsley flakes
1 teaspoon instant chicken bouillon or 1 chicken
  bouillon cube
  Toast points

If using frozen chicken livers, thaw as directed on package or quick-thaw (see note below). Cut livers into halves if necessary.

Melt butter in 8-inch skillet; brown livers over medium heat, stirring occasionally, 3 to 4 minutes. Stir in mushrooms (with liquid) and remaining ingredients except toast points. Heat to boiling. Reduce heat; simmer uncovered, stirring occasionally, until livers are done, about 5 minutes. Serve on toast points. *2 servings.*

Note: To quick-thaw livers, place them in melted butter in skillet. Cover and cook over medium heat until livers are thawed and can be easily separated, about 15 minutes. Remove cover; cook until livers are brown.

TOMATO-GRAPEFRUIT SALAD

1 can (8 ounces) grapefruit sections, drained
1 tomato, cut into wedges
  Salad greens
  Green pepper strips
  Clear sweet-and-sour dressing

Arrange grapefruit sections and tomato wedges on salad greens. Top salads with green pepper strips and drizzle with dressing. *2 servings.*

Variation

Tomato-Pineapple Salad: Substitute 2 pineapple slices for the grapefruit sections and cut tomato into slices.

BUTTERSCOTCH CAKE SUNDAES

2 slices pound cake (from freezer) or leftover
  Gingerbread (page 111) or 2 commercially prepared
  sponge shortcakes
  Vanilla ice cream
  Butterscotch ice-cream topping

Place cake slices on dessert plates; top with scoops of ice cream. Drizzle ice-cream topping on each. *2 servings.*

NESSELRODE SUNDAES

Heat ¼ cup Nesselrode mixture,* stirring occasionally. Soak 2 sugar cubes in orange extract 2 to 3 minutes. Place scoop of vanilla ice cream in each dessert dish. Spoon hot Nesselrode mixture on ice cream. Place a sugar cube on top of each sundae and ignite. *2 servings.*

* Extra Nesselrode? Use as a topping for vanilla, rice or tapioca pudding, lemon sherbet, pound cake or gingerbread. Or make Nesselrode Ice Cream (page 77).

> **Oven-fried Pike**
> **Lemon-Chive Potatoes**
> **Buttered Green Beans**
> **Cabbage-Green Pepper Slaw**
> **Peaches 'n Custard or Spiced Fruit Compote**

OVEN-FRIED PIKE

- 1 **pound fresh or frozen pike fillets**
- 2 **tablespoons butter or margarine**
- ½ **teaspoon salt**
- ¼ **teaspoon pepper**
- ¼ **cup all-purpose flour or buttermilk baking mix**
  Paprika
  Tomato wedges
  Lemon wedges

Heat oven to 500°. If using frozen fillets, thaw as directed on package. In oven, melt butter in shallow baking dish. Sprinkle salt and pepper on fish, then coat with flour and place in baking dish. Sprinkle paprika on fish. Bake uncovered until fish flakes easily with fork, 10 to 15 minutes. Garnish with tomato and lemon wedges. *2 servings.*

LEMON-CHIVE POTATOES

- 1 **can (about 16 ounces) whole potatoes**
- 1 **tablespoon butter or margarine**
- 2 **teaspoons lemon juice**
- ½ **teaspoon freeze-dried chives**

Heat oven to 500°. Drain and rinse potatoes; place in ungreased 1-quart casserole. Cover potatoes with water. Cover and bake until potatoes are hot, 10 to 15 minutes. Drain. Add remaining ingredients and toss until potatoes are coated. *2 servings.*

CABBAGE-GREEN PEPPER SLAW

⅛ **medium green cabbage, cut into pieces**
½ **small green pepper, cut into pieces**
 2 **green onions, cut into pieces**
½ **teaspoon salt**
 2 **tablespoons coleslaw dressing**

Place cabbage, green pepper and onions in blender; cover with cold water. Chop 3 to 5 seconds. Drain thoroughly in colander or sieve. Mix vegetables, salt and dressing. *2 servings.*

PEACHES 'N CUSTARD

½ **cup canned vanilla pudding**
 2 **teaspoons orange juice**
 1 **can (8 ounces) sliced peaches, drained**
 1 **teaspoon currant jelly**

Mix pudding and orange juice; chill. Divide peach slices between dessert dishes. Spoon pudding mixture onto peaches and top each serving with ½ teaspoon jelly. *2 servings.*

SPICED FRUIT COMPOTE

 1 **can (8 ounces) fruit cocktail or fruits for salad**
⅛ **teaspoon allspice**

Heat fruit cocktail (with syrup) and allspice to boiling. Serve warm. *2 servings.*

Hot Tomato Bouillon
Seafood Salad Bowl
Cheese-Onion Twists
Orange Slush
Chocolate Wafers

HOT TOMATO BOUILLON

¾ cup tomato juice
¼ cup water
1 beef bouillon cube

Heat all ingredients over medium-high heat to boiling, stirring occasionally. Serve hot. *2 servings*.

SEAFOOD SALAD BOWL

1 can (4½ ounces) large shrimp, rinsed and drained
1 can (7½ ounces) crabmeat, drained and cartilage removed
6 cups bite-size pieces lettuce (iceberg, Bibb, romaine, leaf)
½ jar (6-ounce size) marinated artichoke hearts, drained
¼ cup sliced pitted ripe olives
1 hard-cooked egg, cut into wedges
½ teaspoon capers, if desired
Freshly ground black pepper
Italian dressing or creamy French dressing

Reserve some shrimp and crabmeat pieces for garnish. Toss remaining shrimp, crabmeat, the lettuce, artichoke hearts and olives. Divide between salad bowls. Garnish with reserved shrimp and crabmeat pieces, the egg wedges, capers and pepper. Serve with dressing. *2 generous servings*.

Note: You can substitute 1 can (about 5 ounces) lobster or 1 can (6½ ounces) tuna for the shrimp or crabmeat.

CHEESE-ONION TWISTS

2 teaspoons instant minced onion
1 tablespoon butter or margarine, softened
2 tablespoons shredded Cheddar cheese
½ cup buttermilk baking mix
2 tablespoons water
  Soft butter or margarine
  Caraway seed, dill weed or poppy seed

Heat oven to 425°. Mix onion, 1 tablespoon butter and the cheese. Stir baking mix and water with fork to soft dough. Turn onto lightly floured cloth-covered board; smooth dough into ball and knead about 5 times. Pat or roll into rectangle, 8x6 inches.

Spread onion mixture on rectangle to within 2 inches of one long side. Beginning with plain side, fold lengthwise into thirds; press together. Cut crosswise into 6 strips. Twist each strip twice.

- Place twists on ungreased baking sheet; press ends on sheet to fasten securely. Brush soft butter on twists; sprinkle with caraway seed. Bake until light brown, about 10 minutes. Serve warm. *6 twists*.

ORANGE SLUSH

In blender or small mixer bowl, mix 1 pint vanilla ice cream, softened, and ¼ cup frozen orange juice concentrate (thawed) until thick and smooth. Garnish each drink with orange slice and mint leaves. Serve with straws. *2 servings*.

Broiled Lamb Patties
Broiled Eggplant with Tomato Sauce
Wilted French Onion Salad
Warm Apricot Crunch Sundaes

BROILED LAMB PATTIES

2 **lamb patties (4 ounces each)**
 Salt
 Lemon pepper

Set oven control at broil and/or 550°. Place patties on rack in broiler pan. Broil with tops 3 to 5 inches from heat until brown, about 7 minutes. Sprinkle with salt and lemon pepper. Turn patties; broil until medium done, about 7 minutes. *2 servings.*

BROILED EGGPLANT WITH TOMATO SAUCE

1 **small eggplant (about 1 pound), pared and cut into ½-inch slices**
 Soft butter or margarine
 Salt and pepper
1 **can (8 ounces) tomato sauce**
¼ **teaspoon garlic powder**

Set oven control at broil and/or 550°. Place eggplant slices on rack in broiler pan. Brush butter on slices; season with salt and pepper. Broil with tops about 3 inches from heat until eggplant is hot and tender, about 6 minutes.

In small saucepan, heat tomato sauce and garlic powder, stirring occasionally. Serve on eggplant slices. *2 servings.*

WILTED FRENCH ONION SALAD

1 small onion, thinly sliced and separated into rings
2 to 4 cups bite-size pieces romaine
¼ cup oil-and-vinegar dressing
2 teaspoons sugar
½ teaspoon instant beef bouillon
Dash red pepper sauce
Grated Parmesan or Swiss cheese
Seasoned croutons

Toss onion rings and romaine in salad bowls. In small saucepan, heat dressing, sugar, bouillon and red pepper sauce to boiling, stirring occasionally. Drizzle hot dressing on salads; sprinkle with cheese and croutons. *2 servings.*

WARM APRICOT CRUNCH SUNDAES

1 can (8 ounces) apricot halves, drained
2 tablespoons brown sugar
¼ cup cashew halves
1 tablespoon soft butter or margarine
Vanilla ice cream

Set oven control at broil and/or 550°. Place apricots in 8-inch ovenproof skillet or shallow baking dish. Sprinkle sugar and cashews on apricots; dot with butter. Broil with tops about 6 inches from heat until sugar and butter are melted and sauce is bubbly, about 2 minutes. Serve immediately on ice cream. *2 servings.*

Dixie Bake with Buttermilk Biscuits
Succotash
Cranberry-Pineapple Salad
Chocolate-Cinnamon Ice Cream

DIXIE BAKE WITH BUTTERMILK BISCUITS

- **1** can (12 ounces) pork luncheon meat
- **12** whole cloves
- **¼** cup apricot preserves
- **1** teaspoon water
- **¼** teaspoon dry mustard
- **1** cup buttermilk baking mix
- **¼** cup water

Heat oven to 425°. Score top of meat, cutting 12 squares or diamonds 1 inch deep. Insert clove in each square. Place meat in ungreased baking pan, 8x8x2 inches, pushing meat to one side of pan. Mix preserves, 1 teaspoon water and the mustard; spoon on meat.

Stir baking mix and ¼ cup water with fork to a soft dough. Turn onto floured cloth-covered board; smooth dough into ball and knead 5 times. Roll dough ½ inch thick. Cut into five 2-inch biscuits; place in pan with meat. Bake until biscuits are golden brown and meat is hot, 15 to 20 minutes. *2 servings*.

Time-saver: Forget all about kneading and rolling the dough. Instead, drop by spoonfuls (5) right into the pan.

SUCCOTASH

½ **package (10-ounce size) frozen corn and lima beans**
¼ **teaspoon salt**
   Dash pepper
2 **tablespoons light cream**
1 **tablespoon butter or margarine**

Cook corn and lima beans as directed except—use only half the amounts of water and salt called for on package. Drain. Add remaining ingredients; heat, stirring occasionally, until butter is melted. *2 servings.*

CRANBERRY-PINEAPPLE SALAD

1 **can (8 ounces) jellied cranberry sauce, cut into ¼-inch slices**
1 **can (8½ ounces) sliced pineapple, drained**
   Crisp salad greens

Arrange cranberry and pineapple slices on salad greens. Serve with mayonnaise or salad dressing if you like. *2 servings.*

Variation

Cranberry-Orange Salad: Substitute 1 orange, pared and cut into ¼-inch slices, for the pineapple.

CHOCOLATE-CINNAMON ICE CREAM

Soften 1 pint chocolate ice cream slightly; stir in ½ teaspoon cinnamon. Spoon ice cream into original container, refrigerator tray or dessert dishes and freeze until firm. *2 servings.*

SOMETHING TO KNOW ABOUT . . .

Pork luncheon meat can be scored to form diamonds, as shown here, or squares. Insert a clove in each diamond to make something simple look like something special.

Pineapple Burgers
Noodles Almondine
Lettuce Wedges with Favorite Dressing
Herbed Crusty Rolls
Chocolate-Peanut Butter Sundaes

PINEAPPLE BURGERS

½ pound ground beef
½ teaspoon salt
 2 canned pineapple slices, well drained*
 2 tablespoons brown sugar
 2 tablespoons catsup
 2 teaspoons prepared mustard

Set oven control at broil and/or 550°. Shape meat into 4 thin patties; sprinkle with salt. Place pineapple slice on each of 2 patties. Top with remaining patties and press edges together to seal.

Place patties on rack in broiler pan. Broil with tops 4 inches from heat until brown, 3 to 5 minutes. Mix brown sugar, catsup and mustard. Turn patties; spoon brown sugar mixture on patties and broil until of desired doneness, 3 to 5 minutes. *2 servings.*

* Extra pineapple slices? Serve as fruit for tomorrow's breakfast. Or use in Broiled Ham and Sweet Potatoes (page 20) or Tomato-Pineapple Salad (page 25).

NOODLES ALMONDINE

Measure contents of 1 package (6 ounces) noodles almondine; divide in half (approximately 1 cup noodles and 3 tablespoons Seasoned Sauce Mix).* Cook half the noodles in 3 cups boiling salted water until tender, about 5 minutes. Drain noodles and return to saucepan.

Stir in 3 tablespoons Seasoned Sauce Mix and half the amounts of butter and hot water called for on package. Heat to boiling, stirring frequently. Reduce heat; simmer, stirring occasionally, until thickened, 8 to 10 minutes. Sprinkle half the almonds on top. *2 servings.*

* To store remaining mix, close package securely; use within 2 weeks. Serve Noodles Almondine with ham, salmon, veal cutlets, chicken or hamburgers.

HERBED CRUSTY ROLLS

Set oven control at broil and/or 550°. Split 2 hard rolls horizontally. Spread soft butter or margarine on halves and sprinkle with Italian herb seasoning. Place on rack in broiler pan. Broil with tops 4 inches from heat until golden brown, about 4 minutes. *2 servings.*

CHOCOLATE-PEANUT BUTTER SUNDAES

Mix 2 tablespoons peanut butter and ¼ cup chocolate syrup until smooth. Serve on scoops of vanilla ice cream. *2 servings.*

Variations

Honey-Peanut Butter Sundaes: Substitute ¼ cup honey for the chocolate syrup.

Hot Chocolate-Mocha Sundaes: Omit peanut butter; heat chocolate syrup with ¼ teaspoon powdered instant coffee.

London Broil
Mushroom Rice
Crisp Green Salad
Fresh Fruit and Cheese

LONDON BROIL

Score 1-pound flank steak; place in shallow glass dish. Pour ½ cup Italian dressing on steak. Cover and refrigerate at least 8 hours, turning meat occasionally.

Remove steak; reserve dressing. Set oven control at broil and/or 550°. Broil steak with top 3 to 4 inches from heat until medium rare, about 4 minutes on each side, brushing with reserved dressing several times. Cut meat across grain at a slanted angle into thin slices. *2 generous servings*.

MUSHROOM RICE

   Uncooked instant rice (enough for 2 servings)
 1 teaspoon butter or margarine
 1 can (2 ounces) mushroom stems and pieces, drained
 ¼ teaspoon parsley flakes

Cook rice as directed on package. Stir in butter, mushrooms and parsley flakes; heat through, stirring occasionally. *2 servings*.

FRESH FRUIT AND CHEESE

Serve a variety of fresh fruit and dessert cheeses (Gourmandise, Port du Salut, Swiss, Bel Paese, Cheddar, Gruyère, Edam, Gouda) on tray with dessert plates and small knives. Cheeses should be at room temperature.

BONUS MAIN DISHES

CURRIED CHICKEN À L'ASPARAGUS

    1 package (9 ounces) frozen small onions with cream
      sauce
    1 jar (5 ounces) boned chicken, cut up, or ¾ cup
      cut-up cooked chicken
    ½ to 1 teaspoon curry powder
    ½ teaspoon seasoned salt
    1 package (10 ounces) frozen asparagus spears
      Toast points

Cook onions as directed on package. Stir in chicken, curry powder and seasoned salt. Heat to boiling. Reduce heat; cover and simmer until chicken is hot, about 5 minutes.

While chicken mixture simmers, cook asparagus spears as directed on package. Place asparagus spears on toast; spoon chicken curry on top. *2 servings.*

Variations

Curried Tuna à l'Asparagus: Substitute 1 can (6½ ounces) tuna, drained, for the chicken.

Curried Turkey à l'Asparagus: Substitute ¾ cup cut-up cooked turkey for the chicken.

Perfect with spiced crab apples and a tossed green salad. Serve peanut butter cookies or coconut macaroons for dessert.

15-MINUTE SPECIAL

    ½ pound ground beef
    1 can (15 ounces) Spanish rice
    ⅛ teaspoon garlic salt
    ¼ teaspoon salt
      Dash red pepper sauce

In 8-inch skillet, cook and stir meat until brown. Drain off fat. Stir in Spanish rice, garlic salt, salt and red pepper sauce. Cook, stirring occasionally, until hot, about 5 minutes. If desired, garnish with parsley. *2 servings*.

Quick go-alongs: Cucumber-Iceberg Salad (page 128), ripe olives, corn chips and pineapple sherbet.

MEATBALL STEW

1 can (15¼ ounces) meatballs in brown gravy
1 can (8 ounces) stewed tomatoes
1 package (8 ounces) frozen mixed vegetables in onion sauce
1 can (8 ounces) whole potatoes
1 teaspoon chili powder
¼ cup water

Combine all ingredients in large saucepan. Heat to boiling, stirring occasionally. Reduce heat; cover and simmer 10 minutes. *2 servings*.

Try this with Garlic Bun Sticks (page 112), Apple Slaw (page 17) and Spicy Raisin Cupcakes (page 108).

TUNA AND CHIPS

1 can (8 ounces) green peas, drained (reserve liquid)
Milk
½ can (10½-ounce size) condensed cream of mushroom soup
1 can (6½ ounces) tuna, drained and flaked
1 tablespoon finely chopped onion
¾ cup crushed potato chips

Heat oven to 350°. Measure reserved liquid from peas and add enough milk to measure ⅓ cup. Mix liquid and soup in ungreased 1-quart casserole. Stir in tuna, peas, onion and ½ cup of the potato chips. Sprinkle remaining potato chips on top. Bake until hot, 25 to 30 minutes. *2 servings*.

Delicious with Tomato-Grapefruit Salad (page 25), whole wheat bread and brownies topped with peppermint ice cream.

JIFFY LOBSTER NEWBURG

1 can (5 ounces) lobster, drained
1 can (10½ ounces) condensed cream of shrimp soup
½ cup milk
2 tablespoons sherry or 2 teaspoons lemon juice
2 or 3 slices toast

Break lobster meat into pieces. Heat soup and milk, stirring occasionally. Stir in lobster; cook over low heat until heated through. Stir in sherry. Serve on toast. *2 servings*.

For a special meal when time is short, serve this with Lemon-buttered Broccoli (page 96), Orange-Bermuda Onion Salad (page 185) and Mocha Parfaits (page 86).

Variation

Jiffy Shrimp Newburg: Substitute 1 can (4½ or 5 ounces) shrimp, rinsed and drained, for the lobster.

ITALIAN BEEF AND NOODLES

½ pound ground beef
½ jar (15-ounce size) meatless spaghetti sauce
  (about ¾ cup)*
¾ cup water
¼ teaspoon instant minced garlic
¼ teaspoon oregano leaves
2 ounces uncooked medium noodles (1 cup)
¼ cup sliced pitted ripe olives
⅓ cup shredded Cheddar cheese

In 8-inch skillet, cook and stir meat until brown. Drain off fat. Stir in remaining ingredients except cheese; heat to boiling. Reduce heat; cover and simmer until noodles are tender, about 15 minutes. Stir in cheese; cover and simmer 5 minutes. *2 servings*.

* Leftover spaghetti sauce? Cover tightly and store in refrigerator; use within 2 or 3 days. Heat and serve on hot cooked spaghetti or other pasta. Good with hamburgers, meatballs, meat loaf and chicken.

Complete the menu with a tossed zucchini salad, bread sticks and Pears au Chocolat (page 19).

SPEEDY STROGANOFF STEW

    1 can (24 ounces) beef stew
    ¼ cup dairy sour cream
    ⅛ teaspoon nutmeg

Simmer stew in saucepan until hot, about 10 minutes. Stir in sour cream and nutmeg. *2 servings.*

Serve with a simple salad of pickled beets and onion rings, warm rye bread and Southern Ambrosia (page 44).

Variation

Speedy Burgundy Stew: Omit sour cream; add ¼ cup red Burgundy to stew before simmering.

DELI CHICKEN

Heat oven to 325°. Split 1 barbecued chicken into halves. Arrange halves skin sides up on ovenproof platter or in ungreased baking pan, 8x8x2 or 9x9x2 inches. Brush each half with 1 tablespoon Caesar dressing, sweet-and-sour sauce, orange marmalade, Italian dressing or barbecue sauce. Bake uncovered until hot and glazed, 15 to 20 minutes. *2 servings.*

DELI-MEXICALI CHICKEN

    1 can (8 ounces) stewed tomatoes or tomato sauce
    ⅛ teaspoon instant minced garlic
    1 teaspoon chili powder
    1 barbecued chicken
    ¼ cup shredded Cheddar cheese

Heat oven to 325°. In ungreased baking pan, 8x8x2 or 9x9x2 inches, mix tomatoes, garlic and chili powder. Split chicken into halves; arrange halves skin sides up on tomatoes. Sprinkle cheese on chicken. Bake uncovered until chicken is hot and cheese is melted, about 20 minutes. *2 servings.*

DELI FIX-UPS

Chicken Casserole

1 pint chicken salad
2 tablespoons shredded Cheddar or Swiss cheese
  Seasoned croutons

Heat oven to 350°. Place salad in ungreased shallow 2-cup casserole; sprinkle cheese and croutons on top. Bake uncovered until hot, about 20 minutes. *2 servings.*

Fruited Chicken Salad

1 pint chicken salad
2 oranges, pared and sectioned
2 tablespoons orange juice
¼ teaspoon ginger
¼ teaspoon salt
  Chopped nuts

Mix all ingredients except nuts in bowl; sprinkle nuts on top. *2 servings.*

Chicken-Vegetable Salad

1 pint chicken salad
1 can (8 ounces) green beans, drained
2 tablespoons sliced stuffed olives
¼ teaspoon salt
  Celery seed

Mix salad, beans, olives and salt in bowl; sprinkle celery seed on top. *2 servings.*

Dilled Shrimp Salad

½ package (10-ounce size) frozen green peas
1 pint shrimp-macaroni salad
¼ teaspoon salt
¼ to ½ teaspoon dill weed
1 hard-cooked egg, cut into wedges

Rinse frozen peas under running cold water to separate and remove ice glaze. Mix peas, salad, salt and dill weed in bowl; arrange egg wedges on top. *2 servings.*

EVERYDAY FAVORITES

**Dinners that make tried-and-true
seem suddenly new**

**Lemon Barbecued Pork Chops
Corn on the Cob
Lettuce Wedges with Roquefort Dressing
Hot Rolls
Apple Crisp**

LEMON BARBECUED PORK CHOPS

- 2 pork loin or rib chops, ¾ to 1 inch thick
- ½ teaspoon salt
- 2 thin slices onion
- 2 thin slices lemon
- 2 tablespoons brown sugar
- 2 tablespoons catsup

Heat oven to 350°. Trim excess fat from chops. Place chops in ungreased baking pan, 8x8x2 inches; season with salt. Top each chop with 1 slice onion, 1 slice lemon, 1 tablespoon sugar and 1 tablespoon catsup. Cover tightly with aluminum foil and bake 30 minutes. Uncover; baste chops and bake until done, about 30 minutes. *2 servings.*

CORN ON THE COB

In large saucepan, heat enough water to boiling to cover 2 to 4 ears. Do not add salt—salt toughens corn.

If desired, add 1 teaspoon sugar and 1 teaspoon lemon juice for each 2 quarts water. Drop corn carefully into boiling water. Cover and cook 5 to 8 minutes, depending on size of corn. Drain. Serve with butter, salt and pepper. For variety, try one of these other favorite seasonings mixed with soft butter: basil, cayenne red pepper, celery seed, chili powder or rosemary leaves. *2 servings.*

LETTUCE WEDGES WITH ROQUEFORT DRESSING

½ **cup dairy sour cream**
¼ **cup crumbled Roquefort or blue cheese (about 1 ounce)**
½ **teaspoon lemon juice**
¼ **teaspoon salt**
 2 **lettuce wedges**

Mix all ingredients except lettuce wedges. Cover and refrigerate at least 1 hour to blend flavors. Add small amount milk or light cream if necessary for proper consistency. Spoon onto lettuce wedges. *2 servings.*

APPLE CRISP

 2 **cups sliced pared tart apples (2 medium)**
 1 **tablespoon water**
½ **teaspoon lemon juice**
½ **teaspoon cinnamon**
¼ **cup granulated sugar or brown sugar (packed)**
 3 **tablespoons flour**
 2 **tablespoons butter or margarine**

Heat oven to 350°. Place apple slices in ungreased 1¾-cup casserole. Sprinkle water, lemon juice and cinnamon on apples. Mix remaining ingredients until crumbly; sprinkle on apples. Bake uncovered until apples are tender and topping is golden brown, about 30 minutes. Serve warm. Top with light cream or ice cream if you like. *2 servings.*

French Onion Soup
Shrimp Creole
Fluffy White Rice
Tossed Green Salad
French Bread
Southern Ambrosia
Praline Squares

SHRIMP CREOLE

    2 tablespoons butter or margarine
  ¾ cup chopped onion
  ½ cup chopped celery
    1 medium green pepper, chopped (about ½ cup)
    1 small clove garlic, minced, or ⅛ teaspoon instant
      minced garlic
    1 can (8 ounces) tomato sauce
  ½ cup water
    1 teaspoon parsley flakes or snipped parsley
  ½ teaspoon salt
  ⅛ teaspoon cayenne red pepper
    1 bay leaf, crushed
    1 package (7 ounces) frozen cleaned raw shrimp*
      (about 1 cup)
1½ cups hot cooked rice

Melt butter in 8-inch skillet; cook and stir onion, celery, green pepper and garlic over medium heat until onion is tender. Stir in tomato sauce, water, parsley flakes and seasonings. Simmer uncovered 20 minutes, stirring occasionally. Stir in frozen shrimp; heat to boiling. Reduce heat; cover and simmer until shrimp are done, about 10 minutes. Serve on rice. *2 servings.*

*Rinse frozen shrimp under running cold water to remove ice glaze before adding to sauce.

SOUTHERN AMBROSIA

Sprinkle confectioners' sugar and flaked coconut on orange slices.

PRALINE SQUARES

¼ **cup shortening or salad oil**
1 **cup brown sugar (packed)**
1 **egg**
1 **teaspoon vanilla**
¾ **cup all-purpose flour***
1 **teaspoon baking powder**
½ **teaspoon salt**
½ **cup chopped nuts**

Heat oven to 350°. Grease baking pan, 8x8x2 inches. Melt shortening in saucepan over low heat. Remove from heat; mix in sugar, egg and vanilla. Stir in remaining ingredients. Spread in pan. Bake 25 minutes. While warm, cut into 2-inch squares. *16 squares.*

*If using self-rising flour, omit baking powder and salt.

SOMETHING TO KNOW ABOUT...

No matter what part of the country you live in, no matter what time of year it is, you can always find shrimp in one form or another.

Raw shrimp in the shell, sometimes called green shrimp, can be purchased fresh or frozen. They're also available shelled and deveined. Or you can buy shrimp that are already cleaned and cooked—canned or frozen in packages.

For every 1 cup cleaned cooked shrimp your recipe calls for, you can

☐ prepare 1 package (7 ounces) frozen peeled shrimp or . . .

☐ prepare ¾ pound fresh or frozen raw shrimp (in shells) or . . .

☐ use 1 can (4½ or 5 ounces) shrimp.

> Oven-fried Chicken
> Parsleyed New Potatoes
> Asparagus Almondine
> Crisp Vegetable Relishes
> Strawberry Shortcake

OVEN-FRIED CHICKEN

¼ cup shortening (part butter) or salad oil
¼ cup all-purpose flour
½ teaspoon salt
⅛ teaspoon paprika
⅛ teaspoon pepper
1½ pounds chicken pieces or 2-pound broiler-fryer chicken, cut into quarters

Heat oven to 425°. In oven, melt shortening in baking pan, 9x9x2 inches or 11¾x7½x1½ inches. Mix flour, salt, paprika and pepper in plastic or paper bag; shake chicken, 2 or 3 pieces at a time, in bag until coated.

Place chicken skin side down in pan. Bake uncovered 30 minutes. Turn chicken; bake until tender, 15 to 20 minutes longer. *2 servings.*

PARSLEYED NEW POTATOES

1 pound new potatoes (6 to 8 small)
2 tablespoons butter or margarine
1 to 2 tablespoons snipped parsley

Scrub unpared potatoes lightly with vegetable brush. Heat 1 inch salted water (1 teaspoon salt to 1 cup water) to boiling. Add potatoes. Cover and heat to boiling; cook until tender, 20 to 25 minutes. Drain. Add butter; toss until potatoes are coated. Sprinkle with parsley. *2 servings.*

ASPARAGUS ALMONDINE

1 package (10 ounces) frozen asparagus spears
1 tablespoon butter or margarine
2 tablespoons diced roasted almonds

Cook asparagus spears as directed on package. Drain. Turn into serving dish; dot with butter and sprinkle almonds on top. *2 servings.*

STRAWBERRY SHORTCAKE

1 pint fresh strawberries
⅓ to ½ cup sugar
1 cup buttermilk baking mix
¼ cup milk
1 tablespoon sugar
1 tablespoon butter or margarine, melted

Slice strawberries into bowl. Sprinkle ⅓ to ½ cup sugar on berries and let stand about 1 hour.

Heat oven to 425°. Mix remaining ingredients with fork to a soft dough. Turn dough onto lightly floured cloth-covered board; smooth dough into ball and knead 8 to 10 times. Roll ½ inch thick. Cut into two 3-inch circles. Place on ungreased baking sheet. Bake 10 to 12 minutes.

Split warm shortcakes; spoon strawberries between layers and on top. Serve with sweetened whipped cream if desired. *2 servings.*

Variation

Peach-Praline Shortcake: Omit strawberries and sugar. Before baking, brush soft butter or margarine on circles; sprinkle brown sugar on tops. Fill and top shortcakes with sweetened sliced peaches.

Hearty Ham Steak
Grilled Sweet Potatoes
Peas Almondine in Foil
Corn Muffins from the Grill
Banana Boats

HEARTY HAM STEAK

2 tablespoons prepared mustard
2 tablespoons pineapple juice or other fruit juice
1 tablespoon brown sugar
1 teaspoon horseradish
   Dash salt
1 fully cooked ham slice, about ¾ inch thick

Combine all ingredients except ham slice in small saucepan; heat to boiling, stirring occasionally.

Place ham on grill 4 inches from medium coals. Cook until hot and glazed, about 5 minutes on each side, basting frequently with mustard mixture. *2 servings*.

GRILLED SWEET POTATOES

Pare 2 sweet potatoes; cut diagonally into ½-inch slices. Cook slices in 1 inch boiling water 10 minutes. Drain. Mix 2 tablespoons butter or margarine, melted, and ¼ teaspoon salt.

Place potato slices on grill 4 inches from medium coals. Cook 10 minutes on each side, brushing frequently with butter mixture. Sprinkle toasted coconut on potato slices. *2 servings*.

PEAS ALMONDINE IN FOIL

1 package (10 ounces) frozen green peas
2 tablespoons slivered almonds
  Salt and pepper
1 tablespoon butter or margarine
1 teaspoon chopped pimiento, if desired

Place frozen block of peas on 18-inch square of double thickness heavy-duty aluminum foil. Sprinkle almonds, salt and pepper on peas. Dot with butter. Wrap securely in foil. Cook directly on medium coals, turning once, until tender, 18 to 20 minutes. Add pimiento just before serving. *2 servings.*

CORN MUFFINS FROM THE GRILL

Bake Quick Corn Muffins (page 61) ahead of time. Split and butter each muffin. Wrap in double thickness heavy-duty aluminum foil. Heat on grill 4 inches from medium coals until hot, about 10 minutes, turning once.

BANANA BOATS

For each serving, cut V-shaped wedge lengthwise in a peeled firm banana. Place on piece of double thickness heavy-duty aluminum foil, 18x6 inches. Fill groove in banana with miniature or cut-up marshmallows and chocolate pieces. Wrap tightly in foil. Cook directly on medium coals about 10 minutes.

SOMETHING SPECIAL...

Yeast Rolls

In medium mixing bowl, dissolve **1 package active dry yeast** in **1 cup warm water** (110 to 115°). Stir in **¼ cup sugar, 1 teaspoon salt, 1 egg, ¼ cup shortening** and **1½ cups all-purpose flour** (if using self-rising flour, omit salt). Beat vigorously with wooden spoon until batter falls from spoon in "sheets." Using first the spoon and then your hands, mix in up to **2¼ cups additional flour**—use just enough so that dough leaves side of bowl almost clean. Since flour

Beat until batter "sheets" from spoon, then add just enough of remaining flour so that dough leaves side of bowl almost clean.

To knead, fold dough toward you and push away with heels of hands in rocking motion, rotate ¼ turn. Repeat until smooth.

To test if dough has doubled in bulk, press 2 fingers into dough; impression will remain if it has risen enough.

absorbs moisture or dries out, depending on the humidity, use only as much as needed. Dough will be rough, lumpy and sticky at this stage. Turn dough onto lightly floured board. Knead until dough is smooth and elastic, about 5 minutes.

Place in greased bowl; turn dough to grease all sides. Cover; let rise in warm place (85°) until double, about 1½ hours.

Punch down dough. Shape rolls (right). Let rise 20 minutes.

Heat oven to 400°. Bake rolls until golden brown, 15 to 20 minutes. *24 Cloverleafs or 32 Crescents.*

Note: To freeze rolls, wrap in heavy-duty aluminum foil (4 in each package), label and freeze. Heat foil-wrapped rolls on rack in 350° oven 20 minutes.

CLOVERLEAFS: Shape the dough into 1-inch balls. Place 3 balls in each greased muffin cup. Brush rolls with soft butter.

CRESCENTS: Divide dough in half. Roll each half into 12-inch circle. Brush with soft butter. Cut into 16 wedges and roll up.

Place rolls with points underneath on greased baking sheet; curve ends slightly. Brush rolls with soft butter.

Puffy Omelet Cahuenga
Maple-glazed Bacon
Marinated Green Bean Salad
Toasted English Muffins
Fresh Fruit Cup

PUFFY OMELET CAHUENGA

  Puffy Omelet (below)
 1 ripe small avocado
 ¾ cup dairy sour cream
 ½ teaspoon salt
 ⅛ teaspoon dill weed
 1 large tomato, peeled, diced and drained

Prepare Puffy Omelet. While omelet bakes, peel and dice avocado. Heat sour cream, salt and dill weed (do not boil). Gently stir tomato and avocado into sour cream mixture; heat through.

To serve, pour part of the sauce on omelet in skillet. Tip skillet and loosen omelet by slipping rubber scraper, pancake turner or spatula under; fold omelet and remove to heated platter. Pour remaining sauce on top. *2 generous servings.*

Puffy Omelet

 3 eggs, separated
 3 tablespoons milk or water
 ¼ teaspoon salt
 ⅛ teaspoon pepper
 1 tablespoon butter or margarine

In small mixer bowl, beat egg whites until stiff but not dry. Beat egg yolks until thick and lemon colored. Beat in milk, salt and pepper; gently fold into egg whites with rubber scraper.

Heat oven to 325°. In 8-inch skillet with ovenproof handle, heat butter until just hot enough to sizzle a drop of water, rotating skillet so that butter evenly coats the bottom. Pour omelet mixture into skillet; level surface gently. Reduce heat; cook until puffy and light brown on bottom, about 5 minutes. (Lift omelet at edge to judge color.)

Place skillet in oven; bake until knife inserted in center comes out clean, 12 to 15 minutes.

MAPLE-GLAZED BACON

½ **pound Canadian-style bacon, cut into ¼-inch slices**
 2 **tablespoons maple-flavored syrup**

Heat oven to 325°. In ungreased small shallow baking dish, overlap bacon slices slightly. Drizzle syrup on slices. Bake uncovered until bacon is hot, about 35 minutes. *2 servings.*

MARINATED GREEN BEAN SALAD

Drain liquid from 1 can (8 ounces) French-style green beans. Pour 2 tablespoons Italian dressing on beans. Cover and refrigerate at least 2 hours. Drain. Serve beans on crisp salad greens and garnish with onion rings. *2 servings.*

FRESH FRUIT CUP

Choose two or more of the following fruits to total 1 to 1½ cups: banana slices; blueberries; strawberries; raspberries; seedless green grapes; peach, pear or pineapple chunks; orange or grapefruit sections or melon cubes. Divide between dessert dishes and top each with ¼ cup orange juice or ginger ale. *2 servings.*

Meat Loaf
Creamy Scalloped Potatoes
Fresh Vegetables Vinaigrette (page 67)
Peach Crisps

MEAT LOAF

   1 egg
   ½ cup milk
   ⅓ cup dry bread crumbs or 1 cup soft bread crumbs
     (about 1½ slices bread, torn into small pieces)
   1 pound ground beef or meat loaf mixture
   2 tablespoons finely chopped onion
   ½ teaspoon salt
   ⅛ teaspoon pepper
   ¼ teaspoon dry mustard
   ¼ teaspoon garlic salt
   1 teaspoon Worcestershire sauce

Mix all ingredients thoroughly. Divide meat mixture in half (about 1½ cups each); shape each into loaf, 5x4 inches. Place both loaves in ungreased loaf pan, 9x5x3 inches, or baking pan, 9x9x2 inches.

Bake in 350° oven about 45 minutes. If desired, top one loaf with catsup, chili sauce or strips of cheese and return to oven for 2 to 3 minutes. Serve this loaf immediately. Cool remaining loaf; wrap in aluminum foil, label and freeze. *2 servings—and 2 for another time.*

Variation

Mini Meat Loaves: Divide meat mixture into 4 equal parts (about ¾ cup each). Spread each in ungreased miniature loaf pan, 4½x2½x1½ inches, or shape into individual loaves and place in ungreased baking pan, 9x9x2 inches. Bake about 35 minutes. Serve 2 loaves immediately. Cool remaining loaves; wrap in aluminum foil, label and freeze.

Note: To serve frozen meat loaf, place foil-wrapped *frozen* loaf or miniloaves on oven rack; heat in 350° oven 50 to 60 minutes.

CREAMY SCALLOPED POTATOES

      2 **tablespoons butter or margarine**
      2 **tablespoons flour**
      1 **teaspoon salt**
        Dash pepper
  1½ **cups milk**
      1 **pound potatoes (about 3 medium), pared and thinly sliced**
      2 **tablespoons finely chopped onion**
      1 **teaspoon butter or margarine**

Heat oven to 350°. Melt 2 tablespoons butter over low heat. Stir in flour and seasonings. Cook over low heat, stirring until smooth and bubbly. Remove from heat. Stir in milk. Heat to boiling, stirring constantly.

In greased 1-quart casserole, layer half the potatoes, all the onion and half the sauce. Top with remaining potatoes and sauce. Dot with 1 teaspoon butter.

Cover and bake 30 minutes. Uncover and bake until potatoes are tender, about 35 minutes. *2 servings.*

PEACH CRISPS

      4 **canned peach halves, drained**
      2 **tablespoons chopped walnuts**
      2 **tablespoons brown sugar**
  1½ **teaspoons finely shredded orange peel**
   ⅛ **teaspoon allspice**
      4 **walnut halves**

Heat oven to 350°. Place peach halves cut sides up in ungreased baking dish. Mix chopped walnuts, sugar, orange peel and allspice; sprinkle on peaches. Bake until hot, about 20 minutes. Serve warm; top each with walnut half and, if desired, vanilla ice cream. *2 servings.*

Baked Meatballs
Oven Rice
Spanish Peppers
Cabbage Slaw (page 121)
Quick Blueberry Cobbler

BAKED MEATBALLS

Prepare mixture for Meat Loaf (page 54) except—decrease milk to ¼ cup. Shape mixture into twenty 1½-inch balls. Place in ungreased baking pan, 9x9x2 inches. Bake in 400° oven about 20 minutes. Serve half the meatballs immediately. Cool remaining meatballs; place in 1-pint freezer container, label and freeze. *2 servings—and 2 for another day.*

Note: To serve frozen meatballs, heat 1 jar (about 15 ounces) favorite spaghetti sauce in 1-quart saucepan to boiling; add frozen meatballs. Reduce heat; cover and simmer until meatballs are hot, about 20 minutes. Serve with hot cooked spaghetti or noodles. Or heat 1 can (10¾ ounces) beef gravy to boiling; add frozen meatballs and heat through. Serve with mashed potatoes.

OVEN RICE

 1 cup boiling water
½ cup uncooked regular rice
½ teaspoon salt
    Snipped parsley

Heat oven to 400°. Mix water, rice and salt in ungreased 2½-cup or 1-quart casserole. Cover tightly; bake until liquid is absorbed and rice is tender, 20 to 25 minutes. Sprinkle parsley on top. *1½ cups rice.*

SPANISH PEPPERS

1 to 1½ green peppers, cut into ½-inch strips
½ cup ¼-inch diagonal slices celery
2 tablespoons finely chopped onion
1 tablespoon salad oil
¼ teaspoon basil leaves
½ teaspoon salt
  Dash pepper
1 can (8 ounces) tomato sauce

In 8-inch skillet, cook and stir green pepper, celery and onion in oil over medium heat until onion is tender. Stir in remaining ingredients. Cover and cook over medium heat until green pepper is crisp-tender, about 5 minutes. *2 servings.*

QUICK BLUEBERRY COBBLER

½ can (21-ounce size) blueberry pie filling*
½ teaspoon shredded orange peel
½ cup buttermilk baking mix
2 teaspoons sugar
2 tablespoons orange juice
2 teaspoons butter or margarine, softened

Heat oven to 400°. Mix pie filling and orange peel in ungreased 2½-cup casserole. Heat in oven 15 minutes. Stir baking mix, sugar, orange juice and butter with fork to soft dough. Drop dough by spoonfuls (2 or 3) onto hot blueberry mixture. Bake until topping is light brown, 15 to 20 minutes. Serve warm, with light cream or ice cream if you like. *2 servings.*

* Leftover pie filling? Serve in Tart Shells (page 119) or use as a topping for vanilla ice cream, lemon sherbet, vanilla pudding, pancakes or French toast.

Orange Pork Chop Skillet
Buttered Peas
Tossed Green Salad
Dinner Rolls
Quick Date Cake

ORANGE PORK CHOP SKILLET

4 pork loin or rib chops, ½ to ¾ inch thick
1 teaspoon salt
1 small onion, sliced
½ can (6-ounce size) frozen orange juice concentrate (thawed)*
2 tablespoons brown sugar
¼ teaspoon allspice
2 tablespoons lemon juice
2 tablespoons water
1 can (8 ounces) sweet potatoes in syrup, drained
1 small orange, sliced

In 10-inch skillet, brown chops over medium heat. Drain off fat. Sprinkle salt on chops. Arrange onion slices on chops. Mix orange juice concentrate, sugar, allspice, lemon juice and water; pour into skillet. Heat to boiling. Reduce heat; cover and simmer 30 minutes. Place sweet potatoes and orange slices on chops. Cover and cook until potatoes are hot, about 10 minutes. *2 servings.*

* Leftover concentrate? Use in Orange Slush (page 29), as an ice-cream topping or for a speedy fruit drink.

TOSSED GREEN SALAD

3 to 4 cups bite-size pieces chilled crisp salad greens
¼ cup vegetables
   Oil-and-Vinegar Dressing (below) or favorite bottled
   dressing

Place greens and vegetables in bowl. Just before serving, pour dressing on ingredients and toss. Garnish
salad as desired. *2 servings.*

Oil-and-Vinegar Dressing

2 tablespoons salad oil
1 tablespoon wine, tarragon or cider vinegar or lemon
   juice
¼ teaspoon salt
½ small clove garlic, finely chopped, or dash garlic
   powder
   Dash freshly ground pepper

Shake all ingredients in tightly covered jar. *About ¼
cup.*

Note: For perfect green salads, use chilled fresh salad
greens. Vary the greens, vegetables and garnishes. Tear
greens into bite-size pieces; do not cut except when
wedges, shredding or chunks are called for. Use just
enough dressing to lightly coat the leaves.

QUICK DATE CAKE

1 package (14 ounces) date bar mix
½ cup hot water
2 eggs
1 teaspoon baking powder
½ cup chopped walnuts
   Confectioners' sugar

Heat oven to 375°. Grease baking pan, 8x8x2 inches.
Mix date filling from date bar mix and hot water. Stir
in crumbly mix, eggs, baking powder and nuts. Spread
in pan. Bake until top springs back when touched
lightly, about 30 minutes. Sprinkle confectioners' sugar
on top.

Southwestern Beef
Buttered Green Beans
Tangy Cauliflower Salad
Quick Corn Muffins
Caramel Custard or Frosty Pumpkin Custard

SOUTHWESTERN BEEF

¾- to 1-pound beef round steak, 1 to 2 inches thick
2 cloves garlic, thinly sliced
1 tablespoon salad oil
½ teaspoon salt
   Dash marjoram or basil
¼ cup water
1 tablespoon butter or margarine
⅓ cup raisins
1 large or 2 small tomatoes, peeled and cut into wedges
   Pickled chili peppers

Cut about 10 small slits in meat with tip of knife; insert a garlic slice in each. Heat oil in 8-inch skillet; brown meat over medium heat, about 15 minutes. Drain off fat. Add salt, marjoram and water; heat to boiling. Reduce heat; cover tightly and simmer until tender, 1 to 1½ hours. (Add small amount of water if necessary.)

Melt butter in small saucepan. Add raisins and tomatoes; cook over low heat, stirring occasionally, until hot, about 5 minutes. Pour around steak and garnish with chili peppers. *2 servings.*

Time-saver: Use ¾-pound beef round steak, ½ inch thick, and omit garlic slices. After browning meat, add salt, marjoram and water; cover and simmer until tender, about 45 minutes.

TANGY CAULIFLOWER SALAD

½ **medium cauliflower**
2 **tablespoons oil-and-vinegar dressing**
¼ **teaspoon oregano**
¼ **teaspoon salt**
  Lettuce leaves

Separate cauliflower into flowerets. Heat 1 inch salted water (½ teaspoon salt to 1 cup water) to boiling. Add cauliflower. Cover and heat to boiling; cook until tender, 10 to 12 minutes. Drain.

Mix dressing, oregano and salt; pour on hot cauliflower and toss. Cover and refrigerate at least 3 hours.

To serve, remove cauliflower with slotted spoon to lettuce-lined bowls. Garnish with finely chopped green onion or grated Parmesan cheese and parsley. *2 servings.*

Time-saver: Substitute 1 package (10 ounces) frozen cauliflower, cooked as directed, for the fresh.

QUICK CORN MUFFINS

Measure 1 package (14 ounces) corn muffin mix; divide in half (approximately 1½ cups).* Prepare muffins as directed except—use half the mix, 1 egg and half the amount of milk called for on package. *6 muffins.*

* To store remaining mix, close package securely and use within 3 weeks to make hot muffins for another meal. Or if you prefer, prepare entire package and freeze leftover muffins to use as needed.

CARAMEL CUSTARD

1 egg, slightly beaten
2 tablespoons sugar
   Dash salt
½ teaspoon vanilla
¾ cup milk, scalded
2 tablespoons caramel ice-cream topping

Heat oven to 350°. Mix egg, sugar, salt and vanilla. Stir in milk. Place 1 tablespoon caramel topping in each of two 6-ounce custard cups. Pour egg mixture onto caramel topping.

Place cups in baking pan, 8x8x2 inches; pour very hot water into pan to within ½ inch of tops of cups. Bake until knife inserted halfway between center and edge comes out clean, 40 to 45 minutes. Remove cups from water; serve warm or chill and unmold into dessert dishes. *2 servings.*

FROSTY PUMPKIN CUSTARD

Line 6 muffin cups with paper baking cups. Soften ½ pint vanilla ice cream slightly. Fold ½ can (16-ounce size) pumpkin pie mix* into ice cream. Divide among paper-lined cups. Cover and freeze until firm, at least 3 hours. Garnish with whipped topping and walnut halves. *2 servings—and 4 for other days.*

* Leftover pumpkin pie mix? Use in Pumpkin Custards (page 166).

> **Herbed Halibut Steaks**
> **Baked Potatoes**
> **Asparagus Pimiento**
> **Crisp Vegetable Relishes**
> **Strawberries and Cream**

HERBED HALIBUT STEAKS

- 1 tablespoon butter or margarine
- 2 tablespoons lemon juice
- 1 package (12 ounces) frozen halibut steaks
- 1 teaspoon onion salt
- ¼ teaspoon lemon pepper
- ¼ to ½ teaspoon thyme, basil or marjoram
  Paprika
  Lemon wedges
  Parsley

Heat oven to 400°. In oven, melt butter in lemon juice in baking pan, 8x8x2 inches. Place frozen fish in pan; turn to coat other side with lemon butter. Sprinkle onion salt, lemon pepper and thyme on fish. Bake until fish flakes easily with fork, about 25 minutes. Sprinkle paprika on fish; serve with lemon wedges and parsley. *2 servings.*

Variation

Herbed Salmon Steaks: Substitute 1 package (12 ounces) frozen salmon steaks for the halibut steaks.

BAKED POTATOES

Heat oven to 400°. Rub 2 medium baking potatoes with shortening if soft skins are desired. Prick with fork to allow steam to escape. Bake until tender, about 1 hour.

To serve, cut crisscross gash in each top; squeeze gently until some potato pops up through opening. Serve with butter or dairy sour cream. *2 servings.*

Savory Beef Stew
Orange and Grapefruit Salad with Ruby-red Dressing
Celery Sticks
Rye Rolls
Chocolate Chip Cookies

SAVORY BEEF STEW

   2 tablespoons shortening
 ½ to ¾ pound beef stew meat, cut into 1-inch pieces
1½ cups water
   1 beef bouillon cube
 ½ clove garlic, finely chopped, or ⅛ teaspoon instant
     minced garlic
 ½ bay leaf, crumbled
   1 teaspoon salt
 ⅛ teaspoon allspice
 ¼ teaspoon lemon juice
   2 small onions or 1 medium onion, cut into quarters
   2 medium potatoes, pared and cut into 1-inch cubes
   2 medium carrots, cut into 1-inch pieces
 ½ package (10-ounce size) frozen green peas*
 ½ cup water
   2 tablespoons flour

Melt shortening in 2-quart saucepan; brown meat. Add
1½ cups water, the bouillon cube, garlic, bay leaf, salt,
allspice and lemon juice; heat to boiling, stirring occasionally. Reduce heat; cover and simmer until meat is
almost tender. 1 to 1½ hours.

Add onions, potatoes and carrots; heat to boiling.
Reduce heat; cover and simmer 20 minutes. Add peas;
cook until vegetables are tender, about 10 minutes.

Shake ½ cup water and the flour in tightly covered
jar until smooth. Stir into stew; heat to boiling, stirring
constantly. Boil and stir 1 minute. *2 generous servings.*

* Leftover frozen peas? Cook as directed on package
and serve as the vegetable in Orange Pork Chop Skillet

menu (page 58) or use in Peas Almondine in Foil (page 49) or Paella (page 196).

ORANGE AND GRAPEFRUIT SALAD

1 orange, pared and sectioned
1 grapefruit, pared and sectioned
  Crisp salad greens
  Ruby-red Dressing (below)

Arrange orange and grapefruit sections in pinwheel design on salad greens. Garnish with maraschino cherry if desired. Serve with Ruby-red Dressing. *2 servings.*

Ruby-red Dressing

Beat ¼ cup currant or cranberry jelly and 2 table-spoons oil-and-vinegar dressing until smooth.

Time-saver: Substitute 1 can (11 ounces) mandarin orange segments, drained, for the orange and grape-fruit.

CHOCOLATE CHIP COOKIES

  ⅓ cup shortening
  ⅓ cup butter or margarine, softened
  ½ cup granulated sugar
  ½ cup brown sugar (packed)
  1 egg
  1 teaspoon vanilla
1½ cups all-purpose flour*
  ½ teaspoon soda
  ½ teaspoon salt
  ½ cup chopped nuts
  1 package (6 ounces) semisweet chocolate pieces

Heat oven to 375°. Mix thoroughly shortening, butter, sugars, egg and vanilla. Stir in remaining ingredients. (For a softer, rounder cookie, add ¼ cup flour.)

Drop dough by rounded teaspoonfuls 2 inches apart onto ungreased baking sheet. Bake until light brown, 8 to 10 minutes. Cool slightly before removing from baking sheet. *About 3½ dozen cookies.*

*If using self-rising flour, omit soda and salt.

Deluxe Baked Chicken
Chili Pepper Casserole
Fresh Vegetables Vinaigrette
Hot Crusty Rolls
Lemon Sherbet with Raspberry-Currant Sauce

DELUXE BAKED CHICKEN

       2 tablespoons salad oil
    ¼ cup all-purpose flour
    ½ teaspoon salt
    ¼ teaspoon paprika
    ⅛ teaspoon pepper
    1½ pounds chicken pieces
    ¼ cup chicken broth
       2 tablespoons sherry or apple juice
       1 small clove garlic, crushed

Heat oil in large skillet. Measure flour, salt, paprika
and pepper into plastic or paper bag. Shake chicken,
2 or 3 pieces at a time, in bag until thoroughly coated.
Brown chicken in oil over medium heat.

Heat oven to 350°. Place chicken skin side up in
ungreased baking pan, 9x9x2 inches. Mix broth, sherry
and garlic. Pour ⅓ of broth mixture on chicken. Cover
with aluminum foil and bake until tender, 45 to 50
minutes, basting occasionally with remaining broth
mixture. Uncover last 5 minutes of baking time to crisp
chicken. *2 servings.*

CHILI PEPPER CASSEROLE

½ can (4-ounce size) peeled green chili peppers*
1 cup shredded process Cheddar cheese (about 4 ounces)
1 egg
½ cup milk
¼ cup buttermilk baking mix

Heat oven to 350°. Grease 2- to 2½-cup casserole. Rinse peppers to remove seeds. Place peppers in single layer in casserole. Sprinkle cheese on peppers. Beat egg thoroughly; beat in milk and baking mix and pour onto cheese. Bake until golden brown and puffy, about 30 minutes. *2 servings.*

* **Leftover chili peppers?** Chop and use as a spicy substitution for pimiento.

FRESH VEGETABLES VINAIGRETTE

1 small zucchini or cucumber, thinly sliced
1 carrot, cut crosswise into ¼-inch slices
¼ cup cauliflowerets
¼ cup oil-and-vinegar dressing
2 lettuce cups

Toss all ingredients except lettuce cups in bowl. Chill at least 2 hours, tossing occasionally. Serve in lettuce cups. *2 servings.*

LEMON SHERBET WITH RASPBERRY-CURRANT SAUCE

1 package (10 ounces) frozen raspberries, thawed
½ cup currant jelly
1½ teaspoons cornstarch
1 tablespoon cold water
½ pint lemon sherbet

Heat raspberries (with syrup) and currant jelly to boiling, stirring frequently. Mix cornstarch and water until smooth. Stir into raspberry-currant mixture. Cook, stirring constantly, until mixture thickens and boils. Boil and stir 1 minute. Cool, and if desired, strain.

Scoop sherbet into dessert dishes. Pour sauce on top. *2 servings.*

Swiss Steak
Mashed Potatoes
Buttered Brussels Sprouts
Apple-Grapefruit Salad with Lime-Honey Dressing
Hard Rolls
Pecan Tarts

SWISS STEAK

¾-pound beef round steak, ½ to ¾ inch thick
2 tablespoons flour
¼ teaspoon salt
⅛ teaspoon pepper
2 tablespoons salad oil
1 can (8 ounces) stewed tomatoes
1 medium green pepper, sliced
1 medium onion, sliced
½ teaspoon salt

Cut meat into 2 pieces. Mix flour, ¼ teaspoon salt and the pepper; coat meat with flour mixture. Heat oil in 8-inch skillet; brown meat over medium heat, about 15 minutes. Add tomatoes to skillet. Reduce heat; cover and simmer 30 minutes. Add green pepper, onion and ½ teaspoon salt. Cover and simmer until meat is tender, 30 to 45 minutes. (Add small amount of water if necessary.) *2 servings.*

APPLE-GRAPEFRUIT SALAD

Arrange unpared red apple slices and grapefruit sections on salad greens. Serve with Lime-Honey Dressing (below).

Lime-Honey Dressing

3 tablespoons frozen limeade or lemonade concentrate (thawed)*
3 tablespoons honey
3 tablespoons salad oil or dairy sour cream
¼ teaspoon celery seed

Beat all ingredients until well blended. *½ cup.*

* Leftover concentrate? Use in Lime Frappé (page 127) or Fresh Fruit Salad (page 97), drizzle it over a fruit cup or stir up a quick fruit drink.

PECAN TARTS

½ stick pie crust mix
1 egg
¼ cup sugar
⅛ teaspoon salt
3 tablespoons butter or margarine, melted
⅓ cup dark corn syrup
⅓ cup pecan halves or pieces

Heat oven to 375°. Prepare pastry for One-crust Pie as directed except—use only half the amount of water called for on package and divide dough in half. Roll each half 1 inch larger than 4-inch tart pan. Ease into pan; flute edge. (Do not prick.)

In small mixer bowl, beat egg, sugar, salt, butter and syrup. Stir in nuts. Pour into pastry-lined tart pans. Bake until filling is set and pastry is light brown, 30 to 35 minutes. Serve warm or cool. Top with whipped cream if desired. *2 tarts.*

No 4-inch tart pans? Use 1 stick or ½ packet pie crust mix. Prepare pastry for One-crust Pie as directed on package except—divide dough into 6 equal parts. Shape each into a ball and roll into 4½-inch circle. Ease into muffin cup or 6-ounce custard cup, making pleats so pastry will fit closely. (Do not prick.) Pour filling into pastry-lined muffin cups. Bake about 30 minutes.

> **Sweet-and-Sour Ribs**
> **Baked Acorn Squash**
> **Chinese-style Cabbage**
> **Rosy Cinnamon Apples**

SWEET-AND-SOUR RIBS

  2 **pounds pork spareribs or back ribs, cut into**
    serving pieces
½ **cup catsup**
  2 **tablespoons brown sugar**
¼ **cup vinegar**
  2 **tablespoons Worcestershire sauce**
  1 **teaspoon celery seed**
½ **teaspoon chili powder**
½ **teaspoon salt**
    Dash pepper
  2 **to 3 drops red pepper sauce**

Place ribs meaty side up on rack in foil-lined shallow
roasting pan. Mix remaining ingredients; pour about
⅓ cup sauce on ribs. Bake uncovered in 350° oven
until done, 1½ to 2 hours, basting 3 or 4 times with
remaining sauce.

For additional flavor and eye appeal, place 1 lemon,
thinly sliced, on ribs during last hour of baking. If ribs
are browning too quickly, cover loosely with aluminum
foil. *2 servings.*

Variation

Pineapple Ribs: Decrease vinegar to 2 tablespoons
and add 1 can (8 ounces) crushed pineapple (with
syrup) to the sauce ingredients.

BAKED ACORN SQUASH

Heat oven to 350°. Cut 1 acorn squash lengthwise in half. Place cut sides down in ungreased baking dish, 8x8x2 inches. Pour water into baking dish to ¼-inch depth. Bake uncovered 30 minutes. Turn squash cut sides up. Dot each half with butter or margarine; sprinkle with salt, pepper, and if desired, 1 tablespoon brown sugar or honey. Bake until squash is tender, 20 to 30 minutes. *2 servings.*

CHINESE-STYLE CABBAGE

    1 tablespoon salad oil
1½ cups finely shredded cabbage
  ½ cup thin diagonal slices celery
  ½ medium green pepper, cut into thin diagonal slices
  ⅓ cup chopped onion
  ½ teaspoon salt
    Dash pepper

Heat oil in 8-inch skillet; add vegetables and mix. Cover tightly and cook over medium-low heat, stirring occasionally, just until crisp-tender, 3 to 5 minutes. Sprinkle with salt and pepper. For extra flavor, add 1½ teaspoons soy sauce just before serving. *2 servings.*

ROSY CINNAMON APPLES

Heat oven to 350°. Core 2 baking apples. Pare upper half of each apple to prevent skin from splitting. Or score skin in petal design. Place apples upright in small baking dish; fill center of each with 1 to 2 tablespoons brown sugar and 1 tablespoon red cinnamon candies. Pour water into baking dish to ¼-inch depth. Bake until apples are tender when pierced with fork, 30 to 40 minutes, spooning syrup on apples several times during baking. Serve warm, with cream or ice cream. *2 servings.*

Barbecued Chicken
Ranch-style Potato Salad
Green Bean-Tomato Vinaigrette (page 101)
Hot Herbed Bread
Strawberry Waffles à la Mode

BARBECUED CHICKEN

Choose a 2- to 2½-pound broiler-fryer chicken, cut into quarters. Season quarters with salt and pepper; place bone side down on grill 5 inches from medium coals. Cook 20 to 30 minutes. Turn; cook until chicken is tender, 30 to 40 minutes, turning and brushing frequently with one of the Sauces (below). *2 generous servings.*

Sauces

French Sauce: Mix ½ cup French dressing and 1 teaspoon celery seed.

Garlic Sauce: Use ½ cup garlic or Italian dressing.

RANCH-STYLE POTATO SALAD

```
   2 medium potatoes
 ⅓ cup sliced celery
 ⅓ cup cubed cucumber
 ¼ cup sliced green onion and top
 ¼ cup thinly sliced radishes
 ½ cup mayonnaise
1½ teaspoons prepared mustard
   1 teaspoon lemon juice
 ½ teaspoon seasoned salt
 ¼ teaspoon celery seed
     Dash pepper
   1 hard-cooked egg, chopped
     Lettuce
```

Heat 1 inch salted water (½ teaspoon salt to 1 cup water) to boiling. Add potatoes. Cover and heat to boiling; cook until tender, 30 to 35 minutes. Drain.

Cool potatoes slightly; peel and cut into cubes (about 1½ cups) into bowl. Add celery, cucumber, onion and radishes. Mix mayonnaise, mustard, lemon juice, seasoned salt, celery seed and pepper; pour on vegetables and toss. Stir in egg. Chill. Serve in lettuce-lined bowl; garnish with tomato wedges and parsley. *2 servings.*

HOT HERBED BREAD

Spread four 1-inch slices French bread with one of the Butter Spreads (below). Place slices together on 18x12-inch piece of heavy-duty aluminum foil. Wrap securely in foil. Heat in 350 to 400° oven or on grill 5 inches from medium coals 12 to 15 minutes. *2 servings.*

Butter Spreads

Cream ¼ cup soft butter or margarine with one of the following:

Garlic: ⅛ teaspoon garlic powder.

Herb-Cheese: 1 teaspoon snipped parsley, ¼ teaspoon oregano leaves, 1 tablespoon grated Parmesan cheese and dash garlic salt.

Italian Herb: ½ teaspoon Italian herb seasoning and dash salt.

Onion: 1 tablespoon minced onion or snipped chives.

Tarragon: 1 teaspoon tarragon leaves and ¼ teaspoon paprika.

STRAWBERRY WAFFLES À LA MODE

2 frozen small waffles, about 3 inches square
  Vanilla ice cream
1 pint fresh strawberries, sliced and sweetened

Heat frozen waffles on grill 5 inches from medium coals until crisp, 3 to 4 minutes on each side. Place scoop of ice cream on each waffle and top with strawberries. *2 servings.*

Canadian-style Bacon
Oven-baked Beans
Mixed Vegetable Salad
Date-Nut Bread
Baked Apples

CANADIAN-STYLE BACON

Place four to six ⅛-inch slices Canadian-style bacon (about ⅓ pound) in cold skillet. Cook over low heat, turning to brown evenly on both sides, 8 to 10 minutes. *2 servings.*

OVEN-BAKED BEANS

  2 slices bacon, diced
  1 small onion, sliced
  1 can (16 ounces) baked beans with pork
  2 tablespoons catsup or chili sauce
  2 tablespoons brown sugar, if desired
  1 teaspoon Worcestershire sauce
  ½ teaspoon prepared mustard

Heat oven to 350°. In large skillet, cook and stir bacon and onion until bacon is crisp. Drain off fat. Stir in remaining ingredients. Pour into ungreased 1-quart casserole. Bake uncovered until hot and bubbly, about 45 minutes. *2 servings.*

MIXED VEGETABLE SALAD

  ½ to 1 cup sliced or diced vegetables
    Oil-and-Vinegar Dressing (page 59) or 3 tablespoons Italian dressing
  1 to 1½ cups bite-size pieces crisp salad greens

Marinate vegetables in dressing 1 to 2 hours. (Here are a few for-instances: raw zucchini, cucumbers, carrots or cauliflowerets; leftover cooked vegetables; canned peas, green beans or mixed vegetables.) Add salad greens and toss. *2 servings.*

DATE-NUT BREAD

½ **cup boiling water**
½ **cup raisins**
½ **cup cut-up dates**
 1 **tablespoon plus 1½ teaspoons butter or margarine**
¾ **teaspoon soda**
¾ **cup plus 2 tablespoons all-purpose flour***
½ **cup sugar**
¼ **teaspoon salt**
 1 **egg**
½ **teaspoon vanilla**
¼ **cup chopped nuts**

Heat oven to 350°. Grease and flour 1-pound coffee can. Pour boiling water on raisins, dates, butter and soda; let stand until cool. Beat in remaining ingredients. Pour into coffee can. Bake until wooden pick inserted in center comes out clean, 60 to 65 minutes. Remove from can; cool thoroughly before slicing.

*If using self-rising flour, decrease soda to ¼ teaspoon and omit salt.

BAKED APPLES

Heat oven to 350°. Core 2 baking apples (such as Rome Beauty, Golden Delicious or Greening). Remove 1-inch strip of skin around middle of each apple or pare upper half of each to prevent skin from splitting.

Place apples upright in small baking dish. Fill center of each apple with 1 to 2 tablespoons granulated or brown sugar, 1 teaspoon butter or margarine and ⅛ teaspoon cinnamon.

Pour water into baking dish to ¼-inch depth. Bake until apples are tender when pierced with fork, 30 to 40 minutes. (Time will vary with size and variety of apple.) If desired, spoon syrup in pan over apples several times during baking. *2 servings.*

Tuna Salad in Tomato Cups
Fresh Vegetable Relishes (page 102)
Popovers
Orange-Pineapple Ice Cream

TUNA SALAD IN TOMATO CUPS

1 can (6½ ounces) tuna, drained and separated into
  chunks
¼ cup chopped celery
2 tablespoons chopped green pepper
1 tablespoon finely chopped onion
½ teaspoon lemon juice
½ teaspoon soy sauce
  Dash white pepper
¼ cup mayonnaise or salad dressing
2 medium tomatoes
  Salt
⅓ cup chow mein noodles or shoestring potatoes
  Celery leaves
  Crisp salad greens

Toss tuna, celery, green pepper, onion, lemon juice, soy
sauce, pepper and mayonnaise in bowl. Cover and chill.

Remove stem ends of tomatoes. Place tomatoes cut
sides down; cut each into sixths, cutting to within 1 inch
of bottom. Spread sections apart to form cups. Sprinkle
salt on sections.

Fold noodles into tuna mixture. Spoon salad into
tomato cups. Garnish cups with celery leaves and place
on salad greens. *2 servings.*

Variations

Ham Salad in Pineapple Boats: Substitute 1 cup cubed
cooked ham for the tuna; omit tomatoes and salad
greens and serve salad in Pineapple Boats: Cut fresh

pineapple lengthwise in half through green top. Cut along curved edges with grapefruit knife; remove fruit and toss with salad. Invert shells to drain.

Crabmeat Salad in Avocado Halves: Substitute 1 can (7½ ounces) crabmeat, drained and cartilage removed, for the tuna; omit tomatoes and salad greens and serve salad in Avocado Halves: Cut unpeeled avocado lengthwise in half; remove pit. Brush halves with lemon juice; sprinkle with salt.

POPOVERS

1 egg
½ cup milk
½ cup quick-mixing flour*
¼ teaspoon salt

Heat oven to 450°. Grease generously 3 deep custard cups (6-ounce size) or 4 medium muffin cups. Beat egg slightly with fork; add milk, flour and salt and stir with fork just until smooth. Do not overbeat.

Fill custard cups ½ full, muffin cups ¾ full. Bake 20 minutes. Lower oven temperature to 350° and bake until deep golden brown, about 20 minutes longer. Immediately remove popovers from cups; serve hot with butter. *3 or 4 popovers.*

*If using regular all-purpose flour, beat ingredients with rotary beater.

ORANGE-PINEAPPLE ICE CREAM

Soften 1 pint vanilla ice cream slightly. Stir in ½ can (6-ounce size) frozen orange-pineapple juice concentrate (thawed). Spoon ice cream into original container or refrigerator tray and freeze until firm. *2 servings.*

Variations

Cinnamon Ice Cream: Substitute 1 teaspoon cinnamon for the concentrate.

Coffee Ice Cream: Substitute 1 to 2 teaspoons powdered instant coffee for the concentrate.

Nesselrode Ice Cream: Substitute 2 tablespoons Nesselrode for the concentrate.

Barbecued Sirloin Steak
Zesty Grilled Potatoes
Fiesta Salad
Corn Chips
Fresh Fruit
Brownies

BARBECUED SIRLOIN STEAK

¾ - to 1-pound boneless sirloin steak, 1 to 1½ inches
  thick
  2 tablespoons olive oil or salad oil
  2 tablespoons wine vinegar
  2 tablespoons sherry or apple juice
  1 teaspoon soy sauce
  ½ teaspoon rosemary leaves
  ¼ teaspoon dry mustard
  ⅛ teaspoon instant minced garlic
  1 tablespoon catsup

Place steak in shallow glass dish. Mix remaining ingredients except catsup; pour onto steak. Let stand about 20 minutes.

Remove steak from marinade with tongs (a fork releases juices); place on grill 4 inches from hot coals. Stir catsup into marinade. Brushing steak occasionally with marinade, grill 1-inch steak 4 to 5 minutes on each side for rare, 7 to 8 minutes for medium, and 1½-inch steak 7 to 8 minutes on each side for rare, 10 to 12 minutes for medium. Make small slit near center of meat to test for doneness. To serve, cut meat across grain at slanted angle into thin slices. *2 servings.*

Variations

Barbecued Cubed Steaks: Substitute 2 cubed steaks (about 4 ounces each) for the sirloin steak and grill 2 minutes on each side.

Barbecued Blade Steak: Substitute blade steak (high quality) for the sirloin steak. Cover and marinate in refrigerator 20 to 24 hours, turning occasionally. Grill until brown on outside and rare in center.

ZESTY GRILLED POTATOES

  2 medium potatoes
¼ cup Italian dressing
½ teaspoon salt
⅛ teaspoon pepper

Heat 1 inch salted water (½ teaspoon salt to 1 cup water) to boiling. Add unpared potatoes. Cover and heat to boiling; cook just until tender, about 30 minutes.

Cut hot unpared potatoes diagonally into ½-inch slices. Place in shallow glass dish; pour dressing on hot slices. Let stand 1 hour, turning slices once.

Remove potato slices and place on grill 4 inches from hot coals. Cook 8 to 10 minutes. Turn; sprinkle salt and pepper on slices and cook until golden brown, 8 to 10 minutes. *2 servings.*

FIESTA SALAD

  1 small onion, thinly sliced and separated into rings
  1 cup coarsely chopped tomato (about 1 medium)
½ cup coarsely chopped cucumber (about ½ medium)
⅓ cup coarsely chopped green pepper (about ½ small)
    Chili powder, if desired
    Oil-and-vinegar dressing

Toss vegetables in bowl; sprinkle chili powder on top. Serve with dressing. *2 servings.*

BROWNIES

 2 ounces unsweetened chocolate
 ⅓ cup shortening
 1 cup sugar
 2 eggs
 ½ teaspoon vanilla
 ¾ cup all-purpose flour*
 ½ teaspoon baking powder
 ½ teaspoon salt
 ½ cup chopped nuts

Heat oven to 350°. Grease baking pan, 8x8x2 inches. In medium saucepan, melt chocolate and shortening over low heat, stirring constantly. Remove from heat. Mix in sugar, eggs and vanilla. Stir in remaining ingredients. Spread in pan.

Bake until brownies start to pull away from sides of pan, 30 to 35 minutes. Cool slightly. Cut into squares, 2x2 inches. If desired, frost with Fudge Frosting (page 89) before cutting. *16 brownies.*

*If using self-rising flour, omit baking powder and salt.

Variation

Peanut Butter Brownies: Decrease shortening to 2 tablespoons and omit nuts. Stir in 2 tablespoons peanut butter and ¼ cup chopped peanuts with the remaining ingredients.

Time-saver: Prepare 1 package (15.5 ounces) fudge brownie mix as directed. For variety, add 1 tablespoon plus 1½ teaspoons powdered instant coffee before mixing ingredients. Or substitute ¼ cup orange juice for the water and add grated peel of 1 orange; frost with favorite orange butter frosting.

Note: Leftover brownies are good for snacks, lunch boxes, picnics. For another day's dessert, serve unfrosted brownies with vanilla, coffee or peppermint ice cream and hot chocolate sauce. Or try a topping of sliced bananas and whipped cream or of cherry pie filling. And then there are Individual Brownie Alaskas (page 7). Brownies freeze well, too.

BONUS MAIN DISHES

CRISPY FISH STICKS

1 package (8 ounces) frozen fish sticks
2 tablespoons French dressing
¼ teaspoon chili powder or barbecue spice
2 teaspoons lemon juice
¼ teaspoon prepared mustard

Arrange frozen fish sticks on ungreased baking sheet. Mix remaining ingredients; brush on fish. Bake or broil as directed. *2 servings.*

Serve with green beans, toast triangles and Orange and Grapefruit Salad (page 65).

TUNA SANDWICH SOUFFLÉ

4 slices bread
1 can (3¼ ounces) tuna, drained and flaked
½ cup shredded natural Cheddar cheese
⅓ cup finely chopped onion
2 tablespoons finely chopped celery
1 tablespoon pickle relish
1 tablespoon mayonnaise
2 eggs, slightly beaten
¾ cup milk
1 teaspoon salt
    Paprika

Heat oven to 350°. Remove crust from bread slices; place 2 slices in greased loaf pan, 9x5x3 inches. Mix tuna, cheese, onion, celery, pickle relish and mayonnaise. Spread on bread in pan and top with remaining bread slices. Mix eggs, milk and salt; pour on sandwich. Sprinkle paprika on top. Bake uncovered until sandwich is golden brown and custard is set, about 45 minutes. *2 servings.*

Tomato slices, tossed salad, chilled pineapple and chocolate cookies make refreshing menu mates.

TUNA-CHEESE STRUDEL

 1 stick or ½ packet pie crust mix
 1 envelope (about 1⅜ ounces) cheese sauce mix
 ½ cup water
 1 can (9¾ ounces) tuna, drained
 1 can (2 ounces) mushroom stems and pieces
 ¼ cup chopped celery
 1 teaspoon instant minced onion
 1 tablespoon milk
 ¼ teaspoon dill weed

Heat oven to 425°. Prepare pastry for One-crust Pie as directed on package except—roll dough into rectangle, 12x9 inches. Place on ungreased baking sheet.

Mix cheese sauce mix and water in medium saucepan. Stir in tuna, mushrooms (with liquid), celery and onion. Heat to boiling, stirring constantly. Boil and stir 1 minute. Cool slightly. Spread tuna mixture lengthwise on center of rectangle, leaving ¾-inch margin at each end. Bring long sides of pastry together at center; press edges and fold over ¼ inch to seal. Turn up ends ½ inch and press. Cut 4 diagonal slits on each side of center seam. Brush milk on pastry; sprinkle dill weed on top. Bake until crust is golden brown, about 20 minutes. *2 servings.*

Complete the menu with creamed peas, Cabbage-Green Pepper Slaw (page 27) and honey-nut sundaes.

SAUERKRAUT PIZZA

 2 cups buttermilk baking mix
 ½ cup water
 ½ cup grated Parmesan cheese
 1 can (8 ounces) tomato sauce
 ½ teaspoon basil
 ½ teaspoon oregano
 ⅛ teaspoon instant minced garlic
 ¾ pound bulk pork sausage, browned and drained
 1 can (8 ounces) sauerkraut, drained
 1 cup shredded Swiss cheese (about 4 ounces)
 ½ teaspoon caraway seed, if desired

Heat oven to 425°. Stir baking mix and water with fork to a soft dough. Turn onto floured cloth-covered board; smooth dough into ball and knead about 1 minute. Roll into 12-inch circle, about ¼ inch thick. Place on ungreased baking sheet or 12-inch pizza pan. Turn up edge ½ inch and pinch or pleat.

Sprinkle Parmesan cheese on circle. Mix tomato sauce, basil, oregano and garlic; spread on cheese. Top with sausage, sauerkraut, Swiss cheese and caraway seed. Bake until crust is brown and topping is bubbly, 20 to 25 minutes. *2 generous servings.*

Simple and satisfying are the keynotes here—needs only a tossed green salad and cherry-nut ice cream.

BAKED CALIFORNIA OMELET

    4 eggs
 ¼ cup dairy sour cream
 ½ teaspoon salt
    1 small tomato, peeled and cut into ½-inch pieces
    1 green onion, sliced
 ¼ cup shredded Cheddar or Swiss cheese

Heat oven to 325°. In small mixer bowl, beat eggs, sour cream and salt on medium speed until well blended, about 1 minute. Stir in tomato, onion and cheese.

Pour into buttered 8-inch pie pan, 8-inch ovenproof skillet, 1-quart casserole or two 1¼-cup baking dishes. Bake uncovered until omelet is set and top is golden brown, 35 to 40 minutes. *2 servings.*

Serve with Orange-Avocado Salad (page 197), toast points and Coffee à la Mode (page 13).

BRAISED PORK CHOPS

    2 to 4 pork loin or rib chops, ½ to ¾ inch thick
    1 teaspoon salt
 ⅛ teaspoon pepper
 ¼ cup apple juice, pineapple juice or water
      Dash Worcestershire sauce

In 10-inch skillet, brown chops over medium heat. Sprinkle salt and pepper on chops. Add apple juice and Worcestershire sauce. Reduce heat; cover and simmer until chops are done, about 30 minutes. (Add small amount of water if necessary.) Serve each chop with a spoonful of Pan Gravy (page 92). *2 servings.*

Down-home flavor is downright easy to achieve with Pecan Sweet Potatoes (page 152), Apple-Celery Toss (page 121) and Ginger Cookies (page 147).

QUICK VEGETABLE SOUP WITH FRANKS

  1 can (10½ ounces) condensed beef broth (bouillon)
½ cup water
  1 clove garlic, finely chopped, or ⅛ teaspoon instant minced garlic
½ teaspoon basil
½ teaspoon monosodium glutamate
½ teaspoon salt
  Dash pepper
  2 carrots, cut into julienne strips
  1 small onion, thinly sliced
  2 frankfurters, cut crosswise into ½-inch pieces
  2 small zucchini, cut into ¼-inch slices
  1 tomato, peeled and cut into eighths, or 1 can (8 ounces) tomatoes

In 2-quart saucepan, combine all ingredients except frankfurters, zucchini and tomato. Cover and simmer 15 minutes. Add remaining ingredients; heat to boiling. Reduce heat; cover and simmer until zucchini is crisp-tender and mixture is heated through, 5 to 7 minutes. *2 servings.*

CANADIAN CHEESE SOUP

½ package (5.5-ounce size) au gratin potatoes*
  2 teaspoons instant chicken bouillon
2¼ cups water
  2 tablespoons finely chopped carrot
  2 tablespoons finely chopped celery
¼ cup light cream
  Snipped parsley

Place potato slices in 2-quart saucepan. Sprinkle sauce mix on slices. Stir in bouillon, water, carrot and celery. Heat to boiling, stirring occasionally. Reduce heat;

cover and simmer, stirring occasionally, until potatoes are tender, about 25 minutes. Remove from heat; stir in cream and sprinkle parsley on top. *2 generous servings.*

* To use half the package, measure contents and divide in half (approximately 1 cup potato slices and 3 table-spoons sauce mix). To store remaining mix, close pack-age securely. Use within 2 weeks to make Hamburger au Gratin Skillet (page 134) or Quick au Gratin Pota-toes (page 18).

QUICK CORN CHOWDER

- 1 can (7 ounces) whole kernel corn with peppers
- 1 can (8 ounces) cream-style corn
- 1 teaspoon instant minced onion
- ¼ teaspoon seasoned salt
- ½ cup light cream or milk
- 1 tablespoon butter or margarine

In small saucepan, heat corn with peppers (with liquid) and remaining ingredients to boiling, stirring occasion-ally. *2 servings (about 1 cup each).*

MORE DIMES
THAN DOLLARS

Inventive dinners that make the most of a little money

Pork Chops Creole
Buttered Green Beans
Peanut Crunch Slaw
Cloverleaf Rolls
Mocha Parfaits

PORK CHOPS CREOLE

- 4 pork loin or rib chops, ½ to ¾ inch thick
- 1 teaspoon salt
- ¼ teaspoon pepper
- 4 thin onion slices
- 4 green pepper rings
- 4 tablespoons uncooked instant rice
- 1 can (8 ounces) stewed tomatoes

In 10-inch skillet, brown chops over medium heat. Sprinkle salt and pepper on chops. Top each with 1 onion slice, 1 green pepper ring, 1 tablespoon rice and ¼ cup tomatoes. Reduce heat; cover and simmer until done, about 45 minutes. (Add small amount of water if necessary.) *2 servings.*

PEANUT CRUNCH SLAW

- 2 tablespoons mayonnaise
- 2 tablespoons dairy sour cream
- ½ teaspoon salt
- 2 tablespoons chopped green onion
- 2 tablespoons chopped green pepper
- ¼ cup chopped cucumber
- 1 cup shredded cabbage
- ¼ cup thinly sliced celery
- 2 tablespoons chopped salted peanuts
  Grated Parmesan cheese

Mix mayonnaise, sour cream, salt, onion, green pepper and cucumber in bowl. Stir in cabbage and celery. Sprinkle peanuts and cheese on each serving. *2 servings.*

MOCHA PARFAITS

- ¼ cup chilled whipping cream or ½ cup frozen whipped topping (thawed)
- 2 teaspoons sugar
- ½ teaspoon powdered instant coffee
- ½ can (18-ounce size) chocolate pudding (1 cup)

In chilled bowl, beat whipping cream, sugar and instant coffee until stiff. (If using whipped topping, omit sugar and mix in instant coffee.) Alternate layers of pudding and whipped cream in parfait glasses or dessert dishes. Chill. Garnish with chocolate shot or chocolate curls. *2 servings.*

SOMETHING TO KNOW ABOUT...

To make chocolate curls, place a large milk chocolate bar on a flat surface. Draw a vegetable parer along the bar toward you, making long, thin strokes. The job will be easier if the chocolate bar is slightly soft. Use a wooden pick to lift the curls so they won't break, as they're fragile.

Broiled Fish and Taters
Buttered Peas
Cabbage Slaw (page 121)
Brown Beauty Cake with Fudge Frosting

BROILED FISH AND TATERS

- 1 pound fresh or frozen cod, perch or flounder fillets
- 2 tablespoons butter or margarine, melted
- 1 tablespoon lemon juice
- 2 tablespoons catsup
- ½ teaspoon Worcestershire sauce
- ½ teaspoon salt
- ⅛ teaspoon dry mustard
- 2 cooked pared medium potatoes, cut into ⅜-inch slices
- 2 tablespoons butter or margarine, melted
- 3 tablespoons grated Parmesan cheese

Thaw fillets if frozen; cut into serving pieces. Set oven control at broil and/or 550°. Place fish on greased rack in broiler pan. Mix 2 tablespoons butter, the lemon juice, catsup, Worcestershire sauce, salt and mustard; brush part of sauce on fish. Broil fish with tops 4 inches from heat 8 minutes, brushing with sauce once or twice. Turn fish; brush with remaining sauce. Arrange potato slices on broiler rack. Brush 2 tablespoons butter on potatoes and sprinkle with cheese. Broil until fish flakes easily with fork and potatoes are golden brown, about 5 minutes. *2 servings.*

Time-saver: No cooked potatoes on hand—and no time to cook them? Use ½ package (14-ounce size) frozen sliced panfried or French fried potatoes instead.

BROWN BEAUTY CAKE

    1 cup all-purpose flour* or cake flour
    1 cup sugar
    ½ teaspoon soda
    ½ teaspoon salt
    ¼ teaspoon baking powder
    ¼ cup water
    ½ cup buttermilk
    ¼ cup shortening
    1 egg
    ½ teaspoon vanilla
    2 ounces melted unsweetened chocolate (cool)
      Fudge Frosting (below)

Heat oven to 350°. Grease and flour baking pan, 8x8x2 or 9x9x2 inches. Into large mixer bowl, measure all ingredients except Fudge Frosting. Blend on low speed ½ minute, scraping bowl constantly. Beat on high speed 3 minutes, scraping bowl occasionally. Pour into pan.

Bake until wooden pick inserted in center comes out clean, 30 to 35 minutes. Cool. Frost with Fudge Frosting.

*If using self-rising flour, omit soda, salt and baking powder.

Fudge Frosting

    ¼ cup shortening
    1 cup sugar
    2 squares (1 ounce each) unsweetened chocolate
    ⅓ cup milk
    ¼ teaspoon salt
    1 teaspoon vanilla

In 2-quart saucepan, heat all ingredients except vanilla to rolling boil, stirring occasionally. Boil 1 minute without stirring. Place pan in bowl of rice and water; beat frosting until cool and of spreading consistency. Stir in vanilla. *Enough frosting for 8- or 9-inch square cake.*

> **Eggs Delmonico**
> **Nutmeg Spinach**
> **Apple-Orange Pinwheel Salad**
> **Coffee Crunch Bars**

EGGS DELMONICO

1 can (10½ ounces) condensed cream of mushroom or
    cream of chicken soup
½ cup shredded natural Cheddar cheese
3 or 4 hard-cooked eggs, sliced
1 tablespoon finely chopped pimiento
    Hot buttered toast or toasted English muffins
    Paprika or snipped parsley

In 1-quart saucepan, heat soup over medium heat until
hot and bubbly, 3 to 5 minutes. Stir in cheese; cook
over low heat, stirring occasionally, until cheese is
melted. Fold in eggs and pimiento; heat through, about
2 minutes. Serve on toast; sprinkle paprika on top.
2 servings.

Variation

Creamed Eggs with Tuna: Use only 2 eggs and fold
in 1 can (3¼ ounces) tuna, drained and flaked.

NUTMEG SPINACH

1 pound fresh spinach
½ teaspoon salt
⅛ teaspoon nutmeg
    Dash lemon pepper
1 tablespoon butter or margarine

Remove imperfect leaves and root ends of spinach.
Wash spinach; drain and place in large saucepan with

just the water which clings to leaves. Cover and cook until spinach is wilted, 3 to 5 minutes. Drain. Stir in salt, nutmeg, lemon pepper and butter. *2 servings*.

Time-saver: Cook 1 package (10 ounces) frozen chopped spinach as directed; drain and season with nutmeg, lemon pepper and butter.

APPLE-ORANGE PINWHEEL SALAD

1 red apple
1 orange, pared and sectioned
Crisp salad greens
Honey Dressing (below)

Cut unpared apple into wedges. Arrange apple wedges and orange sections in pinwheel design on salad greens. Drizzle Honey Dressing on fruit. *2 servings*.

Honey Dressing

Mix ¼ cup mayonnaise or salad dressing, 2 table-spoons honey and 1½ teaspoons lemon juice.

COFFEE CRUNCH BARS

1 cup all-purpose flour*
½ cup brown sugar (packed)
½ cup butter or margarine, softened
2 to 3 teaspoons powdered instant coffee
¼ teaspoon baking powder
⅛ teaspoon salt
½ teaspoon vanilla
¼ cup chopped walnuts
½ cup semisweet chocolate pieces

Heat oven to 350°. Mix flour, sugar, butter, coffee, baking powder, salt and vanilla. Stir in nuts and chocolate pieces. Press mixture evenly into ungreased baking pan, 9x9x2 inches. Bake until light brown and crisp, 20 to 25 minutes. Cut into bars, 3x1½ inches, while warm. *18 bars*.

*If using self-rising flour, omit baking powder and salt.

Country-fried Chicken
Pan Gravy
Mashed Potatoes
Green Peas
Lemon-Fresh Mushroom Salad
Peach-Praline Shortcake (page 45)

COUNTRY-FRIED CHICKEN

Salad oil
¼ cup all-purpose flour
½ teaspoon salt
⅛ teaspoon pepper
⅛ teaspoon paprika
1½ pounds chicken pieces or 2-pound broiler-fryer
chicken, quartered or cut up

Heat ¼ inch salad oil in large skillet. Mix flour, salt, pepper and paprika; coat chicken with flour mixture. Cook chicken in oil over medium heat until light brown, 15 to 20 minutes. Reduce heat; cover tightly and simmer until thickest pieces are tender, 20 to 25 minutes, turning chicken once or twice to assure even cooking. (Add small amount of water if necessary.) Remove cover the last 5 minutes of cooking time to crisp chicken. *2 servings.*

PAN GRAVY

1 tablespoon drippings (fat and juices)
1 tablespoon flour
½ to ¾ cup liquid (broth, milk, vegetable liquid, water)
Salt and pepper

Remove meat to warm platter; keep warm while preparing gravy. Pour drippings into bowl, leaving brown particles in pan. Return 1 tablespoon drippings to pan. Mix in flour. Cook over low heat, stirring until mixture is smooth and bubbly. Remove from heat. Stir in liquid.

Heat to boiling, stirring constantly. Boil and stir 1 minute. If desired, stir in few drops bottled brown bouquet sauce for color. Season with salt and pepper. *½ to ¾ cup.*

LEMON-FRESH MUSHROOM SALAD

¼ pound fresh mushrooms, sliced
Lemon-Herb Marinade (below)
2 lettuce wedges
2 large tomato slices

Place mushrooms in glass dish. Pour Lemon-Herb Marinade on mushrooms; cover and refrigerate up to 12 hours. Place lettuce wedge with tomato slice on each salad plate and top with mushrooms and small amounts of marinade. *2 servings.*

Lemon-Herb Marinade

¼ cup salad oil
¼ cup lemon juice
1 teaspoon seasoned salt
¼ teaspoon marjoram, basil or oregano
⅛ teaspoon sugar
⅛ teaspoon garlic salt
Dash freshly ground pepper

Shake all ingredients together in tightly covered jar. *½ cup.*

SOMETHING TO KNOW ABOUT...

When you stir flour into pan drippings to make Pan Gravy, make sure you scrape in all the brown particles formed by cooking the meat—they're full of flavor and will give the gravy a deep-brown color. Don't forget that Pan Gravy can be made with the drippings of any meat that's been panfried, oven roasted or broiled, from pork chops to the Thanksgiving turkey.

Mexican Steak 'n Beans
Orange-Cucumber Salad
Cornmeal Butter Sticks (page 129)
Hot Fudge-Cinnamon Sundaes

MEXICAN STEAK 'N BEANS

½ pound beef round steak, ½ to ¾ inch thick
1 tablespoon flour
½ to 1 teaspoon chili powder
¼ teaspoon salt
⅛ teaspoon pepper
⅛ teaspoon ground cumin, if desired
1 tablespoon salad oil
½ cup water
¼ cup chili sauce
¾ cup sliced celery
1 medium onion, chopped (about ½ cup)
1 carrot, cut diagonally into ½-inch slices
1 small green pepper, cut into ¼-inch strips
1 can (8 ounces) kidney beans

Cut meat into 1-inch pieces. Mix flour, chili powder, salt, pepper and cumin; coat meat with flour mixture.

Heat oil in 8-inch skillet; brown meat over medium heat, about 10 minutes. Drain off fat. Stir in water, chili sauce, celery and onion; heat to boiling. Reduce heat; cover and simmer until meat is almost tender, 30 to 45 minutes. (Add small amount of water if necessary.)

Add carrot; cover and simmer 20 minutes. Stir in green pepper and beans (with liquid); cover and simmer until green pepper is crisp-tender and beans are hot, about 10 minutes. *2 servings.*

ORANGE-CUCUMBER SALAD

1 orange, pared and sectioned
1 medium cucumber, sliced
1 small onion, sliced and separated into rings
    Orange Dressing (page 197) or French dressing
    Crisp salad greens

Toss orange sections, cucumber slices, onion rings and
Orange Dressing in bowl. Cover and refrigerate 1 to 2
hours. To serve, remove salad with slotted spoon to
salad greens. *2 servings.*

HOT FUDGE-CINNAMON SUNDAES

Prepare Hot Fudge Sauce (below) or heat about ¼
cup commercially prepared chocolate sauce. Spoon
¼ cup hot sauce on scoops of cinnamon or vanilla ice
cream. *2 servings.*

Hot Fudge Sauce

¾ cup light cream (20%) or evaporated milk
1 cup sugar
2 ounces unsweetened chocolate
2 tablespoons butter or margarine
½ teaspoon vanilla
¼ teaspoon salt

Heat cream and sugar to rolling boil, stirring constantly.
Boil and stir 1 minute. Reduce heat; add chocolate and
stir until chocolate is melted and sauce is smooth. (If
sauce has slightly curdled appearance, beat until creamy
smooth.) Remove from heat; stir in butter, vanilla and
salt. *1½ cups.*

Note: Refrigerate leftover sauce in covered container.
To use again, reheat over low heat, stirring constantly.

Salmon Loaf
Lemon-buttered Broccoli
Fresh Fruit Salad with Lime-Honey Dressing
Breadsticks
Hot Fudge Pudding Cake

SALMON LOAF

- **1** **can (8 ounces) salmon, drained (reserve liquid)**
  Milk plus reserved salmon liquid to measure ⅓ cup
- **1** **egg, slightly beaten**
- **¾** **cup cracker crumbs**
- **1** **tablespoon lemon juice**
- **1** **tablespoon chopped onion**
  Dash pepper
  Egg Sauce (below)

Heat oven to 350°. Flake salmon, removing skin and bone. Mix in remaining ingredients except sauce. In buttered baking pan, 8x8x2 inches, shape mixture into a loaf. Bake uncoverd until center is firm, about 30 minutes. Serve with Egg Sauce. *2 servings.*

Egg Sauce

- **1** **tablespoon butter or margarine**
- **1** **tablespoon flour**
- **¼** **teaspoon salt**
- **⅛** **teaspoon pepper**
- **¾** **cup milk**
- **1** **hard-cooked egg, diced**

Melt butter in small saucepan. Mix in flour, salt and pepper. Cook over low heat, stirring until mixture is smooth and bubbly. Remove from heat and stir in milk. Heat to boiling, stirring constantly. Boil and stir 1 minute. Stir in egg. *¾ cup.*

Variations

Cucumber Sauce: Omit egg and stir in ¼ cup shredded or thinly sliced cucumber and dash cayenne red pepper.

Dill Sauce: Omit egg and stir in ½ teaspoon dill weed and dash nutmeg.

LEMON-BUTTERED BROCCOLI

Heat oven to 350°. In ungreased 1-quart casserole, place 1 package (10 ounces) frozen broccoli spears, 1 tablespoon butter or margarine and 2 teaspoons lemon juice. Cover and bake until tender, about 35 minutes. *2 servings.*

FRESH FRUIT SALAD

  1 grapefruit, pared and sectioned
¼ cantaloupe, pared and cut into pieces
  1 cup fresh strawberries, halved
     Lime-Honey Dressing (page 69)
     Lettuce

Toss fruit and dressing. Serve on lettuce. *2 servings.*

HOT FUDGE PUDDING CAKE

⅓ cup all-purpose flour*
¼ cup granulated sugar
  1 tablespoon cocoa
¾ teaspoon baking powder
⅛ teaspoon salt
  3 tablespoons milk
  1 tablespoon salad oil
⅓ cup chopped nuts
⅓ cup brown sugar (packed)
  1 tablespoon cocoa
⅔ cup hot water

Heat oven to 350°. Mix all ingredients except brown sugar, 1 tablespoon cocoa and the hot water. Pour into ungreased 1-quart casserole. Mix brown sugar and 1 tablespoon cocoa; sprinkle on batter. Pour hot water on batter. Bake 30 to 35 minutes. Serve warm. Top with whipped cream or ice cream if you wish. *2 servings.*

*If using self-rising flour, omit baking powder and salt.

Lamb Chops Hawaiian
Fluffy White Rice
Minted Carrots
Tossed Spinach Salad (page 114)
Velvet Crumb Cake with Broiled Topping

LAMB CHOPS HAWAIIAN

   2 **lamb shoulder chops (arm or blade), ¾ to 1 inch thick**
   1 **can (8 ounces) pineapple tidbits, drained (reserve syrup)**
   2 **tablespoons soy sauce**
   2 **tablespoons vinegar**
  ¼ **teaspoon dry mustard**
   1 **tablespoon salad oil**
   2 **tablespoons brown sugar**
  ¾ **teaspoon cornstarch**
1½ **cups hot cooked rice**
     Parsley

Place meat in shallow glass dish. Mix reserved pineapple syrup, the soy sauce, vinegar and mustard; pour on meat. Cover and refrigerate at least 4 hours, turning meat occasionally.

Remove meat from marinade; reserve marinade. Heat oil in 8-inch skillet; brown meat over medium heat. Pour ¼ cup reserved marinade on chops. Cover and simmer until tender, 30 to 40 minutes.

Mix sugar and cornstarch in small saucepan. Stir in remaining reserved marinade. Heat to boiling, stirring constantly. Reduce heat; simmer 2 to 3 minutes. Stir in pineapple; heat through, about 1 minute. Serve chops with pineapple sauce and rice. Garnish with parsley. *2 servings.*

MINTED CARROTS

4 or 5 medium carrots
**1 tablespoon mint-flavored jelly or 1 teaspoon finely
  snipped mint leaves**

Cut carrots lengthwise into ⅜-inch-wide strips. Heat
1 inch salted water (½ teaspoon salt to 1 cup water)
to boiling. Add carrots. Cover and heat to boiling; cook
until tender, about 10 minutes. Drain. Dot hot carrots
with jelly; stir lightly to glaze carrots. *2 servings*.

VELVET CRUMB CAKE WITH BROILED TOPPING

Bake Velvet Crumb Cake as directed on package of
buttermilk baking mix. Spread Broiled Topping (below) on ⅓ of warm cake. Cover remaining cake with
aluminum foil. Broil cake with top 3 inches from heat
until topping is golden, about 3 minutes. *2 servings*.

Broiled Topping

2 tablespoons brown sugar
2 tablespoons soft butter or margarine
1 tablespoon light cream
¼ cup coconut
2 tablespoons chopped nuts

Mix all ingredients.

Note: Wrap remaining cake in aluminum foil (2 servings in each package) and store in refrigerator or
freezer. To serve warm, heat in foil in 400° oven 10
minutes (if frozen, heat 30 to 35 minutes). Top with
apricot or peach jam, cranberry relish, blueberry or
cherry pie filling, fresh or frozen (thawed) strawberries,
Pineapple Sauce (page 106) or vanilla ice cream and
chocolate sauce.

> **Crusty Curried Chicken with Biscuits**
> **Buttered Broccoli**
> **Green Bean-Tomato Vinaigrette**
> **Frosted Melon Wedges with Berries**

CRUSTY CURRIED CHICKEN WITH BISCUITS

   2 tablespoons salad oil
   ½ cup buttermilk baking mix
   1 tablespoon curry powder
   1 teaspoon salt
   ⅛ teaspoon pepper
1½ pounds chicken pieces or 2-pound broiler-fryer chicken, quartered
   1 cup buttermilk baking mix
   ¼ cup water
   2 canned peach halves, if desired

Heat oven to 425°. Pour oil into baking pan, 9x9x2 or 11¾x7½x1½ inches. Mix ½ cup baking mix, the curry powder, salt and pepper; coat chicken with mixture. Place chicken skin side down in pan. Bake uncovered 35 minutes.

Mix 1 cup baking mix and water to a soft dough. Turn chicken, pushing pieces to one side of pan. Drop dough by spoonfuls (5) into pan in single layer next to chicken. Arrange peaches on chicken. Bake until biscuits are light brown and chicken is tender, about 15 minutes. *2 servings.*

Variations

Gaucho Chicken with Chived Biscuits: Substitute 2 teaspoons chili powder for the curry powder; before mixing biscuit dough, add 1½ teaspoons snipped chives to baking mix.

Herbed Chicken with Biscuits: Substitute ¼ teaspoon thyme leaves and ¼ teaspoon rosemary leaves for the curry powder.

BUTTERED BROCCOLI

Trim off large leaves of ¾ to 1 pound broccoli; remove tough ends of lower stems. Wash broccoli. If stems are thicker than 1 inch in diameter, make lengthwise gashes in each stem.

Heat 1 inch salted water (½ teaspoon salt to 1 cup water) to boiling. Add broccoli; cover and heat to boiling. Cook until stems are tender, 12 to 15 minutes. Drain; dot with 1 tablespoon butter or margarine. *servings.*

GREEN BEAN-TOMATO VINAIGRETTE

1 can (8 ounces) cut green beans, drained
¼ pint cherry tomatoes, cut into halves
1 small onion, sliced
1 can (2 ounces) sliced mushrooms, drained
¼ cup Italian dressing

Toss all ingredients together in bowl. Cover and chill at least 2 hours, tossing occasionally. *2 servings.*

FROSTED MELON WEDGES WITH BERRIES

Place scoop of your favorite sherbet in center of each of 2 melon wedges; top each with ¾ cup berries. Here are some combinations you might like:

Honeydew melon, lemon or pineapple sherbet, raspberries or strawberries.

Cantaloupe or Persian melon, orange sherbet, blackberries.

Crenshaw melon, lime sherbet, blueberries or blackberries. *2 servings.*

> **Sausage and Sauerkraut with Dumplings**
> **Fresh Vegetable Relishes**
> **Warm Rye Rolls**
> **Spiced Applesauce à la Mode**
> **Gingersnaps**

SAUSAGE AND SAUERKRAUT WITH DUMPLINGS

    1 can (8 ounces) sauerkraut
    4 medium Polish or bratwurst sausages
   ¼ teaspoon caraway seed
    1 tablespoon chopped onion
   ½ cup water
   ½ cup buttermilk baking mix
    3 tablespoons milk
      Snipped parsley

In saucepan, heat sauerkraut (with liquid), sausages, caraway seed, onion and water to boiling. Reduce heat; cover and simmer 30 minutes.

Stir baking mix and milk with fork to a soft dough. Drop dough by spoonfuls (2 or 3) onto sauerkraut. Cook uncovered over low heat 10 minutes; cover and cook 10 minutes. Remove dumplings, sausages and sauerkraut with slotted spoon to serving platter. Garnish with parsley. *2 servings.*

FRESH VEGETABLE RELISHES

Arrange a variety of vegetables attractively on small tray or in mug. Suggestions include: cherry tomatoes, carrot, cucumber, celery or zucchini sticks; green or red pepper strips or rings. Or prepare any of the vegetable relishes below. Chill until serving time.

Broccoli Buds and Cauliflowerets: Break head of broccoli or cauliflower into bite-size flowerets.

Carrot Curls: With vegetable parer, cut carrot lengthwise into paper-thin slices. Roll up slices and fasten with picks. Place in ice and water. (Remove picks before serving.)

Cucumber Petals: Run tines of fork down length of unpared cucumber. Cut crosswise into very thin slices.

Green Onions: Remove any loose layers of skin. Trim, leaving about 3 inches of green.

Radish Fans: Remove stem and root ends from large radishes. Make thin crosswise cuts almost through radishes. Place in ice and water.

Rutabaga or Turnip Strips: Thinly pare raw rutabaga or turnip; cut into narrow strips or thin slices. For an attractive design, use a lattice cutter.

SPICED APPLESAUCE À LA MODE

1 cup applesauce
½ teaspoon cinnamon
½ teaspoon lemon juice
   Vanilla ice cream

In small saucepan, heat applesauce, cinnamon and lemon juice, stirring occasionally, until hot. Divide applesauce between dessert dishes. Top each serving with ice cream. *2 servings*.

SOMETHING SPECIAL . . .

Kitchen Know-How

To grate lemon or orange peel: Rub fruit on fine part of grater, using short strokes. Grate only outer colored part of peel.

To cut julienne strips: Cut meat or vegetables into narrow lengthwise strips.

To coat chicken, meat or vegetables: Place flour or crumbs in plastic or paper bag. Shake a few pieces at a time.

To peel tomatoes: Dip in boiling water 1 minute. Plunge into cold water. Skin will peel off easily.

To slice mushrooms: Trim off spots; cut off ends of stems. Slice whole mushrooms through stems.

To slice celery or other vegetables: Cut into thin slices on the diagonal for pretty salads and Oriental specialties.

To snip parsley: Cut or break off stems. Place sprigs in glass measuring cup and snip with kitchen shears.

To chop nuts, vegetables or fruits: Hold down point of French knife and rock blade vertically by handle, swiveling from side to side.

To dice onion: Peel. Cut off end slice; cut exposed surface deeply into squares. Cut crosswise into slices, making ¼-inch cubes.

Barleyburger Stew
Hot French Bread
Fresh Vegetable Relishes (page 102)
Velvet Crumb Cake with Pineapple Sauce

BARLEYBURGER STEW

½ pound ground beef
½ cup chopped onion
¼ cup chopped celery
1 can (18 ounces) tomato juice (2¼ cups)
½ cup water
1 teaspoon salt
1 to 1½ teaspoons chili powder
¼ teaspoon pepper
¼ cup uncooked barley

In 3-quart saucepan, cook and stir meat and onion until meat is brown and onion is tender. Drain off fat. Stir in remaining ingredients; heat to boiling. Reduce heat; cover and simmer until barley is done and stew is desired consistency, about 1 hour. *2 servings.*

VELVET CRUMB CAKE WITH PINEAPPLE SAUCE

⅓ cup brown sugar (packed)
2 teaspoons cornstarch
1 can (8½ ounces) crushed pineapple
2 servings Velvet Crumb Cake (page 99) or pound cake or 2 commercially prepared sponge shortcakes

Mix sugar and cornstarch in small saucepan. Stir in pineapple (with syrup). Cook over medium heat, stirring constantly, until mixture thickens and boils. Boil and stir 1 minute. Serve warm sauce on cake. Top with whipped topping or whipped cream if you like. *2 servings.*

Split Pea Soup
Assorted Crackers
Lettuce Wedges with Waldorf Dressing
Spicy Raisin Cake with Browned Butter Frosting

SPLIT PEA SOUP

 2 cups dried split peas
 2 quarts water
 1 pound smoked ham shank or ham hocks or 1 ham
   bone
 1 medium onion, finely chopped (about ½ cup)
 1 cup finely chopped celery
 1 sprig parsley
 ¼ teaspoon pepper
 2 medium carrots, thinly sliced

In large saucepan or Dutch oven, heat peas and water
to boiling; boil 2 minutes. Remove from heat; cover
and let stand 1 hour.

Add ham shank, onion, celery, parsley and pepper;
heat to boiling. Reduce heat; cover and simmer 1½
hours. Add carrots; cover and simmer until carrots are
done and soup is of desired consistency, about 30
minutes.

Remove bone; trim meat from bone and add meat to
soup. For a thinner consistency, stir milk or water into
soup. Season to taste.

Serve half the soup for this meal. Refrigerate remaining soup for the next day. Or pour soup into freezer
container and freeze. *2 servings—and 2 for another
day.*

LETTUCE WEDGES WITH WALDORF DRESSING

½ cup diced unpared red apple
¼ cup seeded Tokay grape halves
2 tablespoons chopped celery
½ cup blue cheese dressing or mayonnaise
   Lettuce wedges

Mix apple, grapes, celery and dressing; spoon on lettuce wedges. *2 servings*.

SPICY RAISIN CAKE

1¼ cups all-purpose flour*
1 cup sugar
1½ teaspoons baking powder
1 teaspoon cinnamon
½ teaspoon salt
½ teaspoon nutmeg
¼ teaspoon cloves
¾ cup milk
⅓ cup shortening
1 egg
1 cup raisins
   Browned Butter Frosting (below)

Heat oven to 350°. Grease and flour baking pan, 8x8x2 or 9x9x2 inches. Into large mixer bowl, measure all ingredients except raisins and frosting. Blend on low speed ½ minute, scraping bowl constantly. Beat on high speed 3 minutes, scraping bowl occasionally. Fold in raisins. Pour into pan. Bake until wooden pick inserted in center comes out clean, 35 to 40 minutes. Cool; frost with Browned Butter Frosting.

*If using self-rising flour, omit baking powder and salt.

Browned Butter Frosting

3 tablespoons butter
1½ cups confectioners' sugar
½ teaspoon vanilla
   About 1 tablespoon milk

In small saucepan, heat butter over medium heat until a delicate brown. Mix into sugar. Stir in vanilla and

milk until frosting is smooth and of spreading consistency. *Enough frosting for an 8- or 9-inch square
cake.*

Variation

Spicy Raisin Cupcakes: Place paper baking cups in
15 or 16 muffin cups. Pour batter into cups, filling each
½ full. Bake 25 to 30 minutes.

> **Skillet Macaroni and Cheddar**
> **Scalloped Tomatoes**
> **Marinated Green Bean Salad (page 53)**
> **Hard Rolls**
> **Gingerbread Stacks with Hot Butterscotch Sauce**

SKILLET MACARONI AND CHEDDAR

    3 tablespoons butter or margarine
    ½ package (8-ounce size) macaroni and Cheddar
       dinner*
    2 tablespoons chopped green pepper
  1½ cups hot water
    ½ to ¾ cup cubed cooked ham or pork luncheon meat
    ⅛ teaspoon dry mustard
    2 tablespoons chopped pimiento, if desired

Melt butter in 8-inch skillet. Cook and stir macaroni
and green pepper over medium heat until macaroni is
light golden, 3 to 5 minutes. Stir in water. Cover and
simmer until macaroni is tender, about 15 minutes. Stir
in meat, Cheese Sauce Mix and mustard. Simmer, stirring constantly, until meat is hot and cheese sauce is
thickened, about 2 minutes. Stir in pimiento. *2 servings.*

* To use half the package, measure contents and divide
in half (approximately ¾ cup macaroni and ⅓ cup
Cheese Sauce Mix). To store remaining mix, close
package securely and use within 2 weeks.

SCALLOPED TOMATOES

1 can (8 ounces) stewed tomatoes
⅛ teaspoon salt
⅛ teaspoon sugar
   Dash pepper
1 teaspoon butter or margarine
⅓ cup seasoned croutons

In small saucepan, heat tomatoes, salt, sugar and pepper to boiling. Reduce heat; cover and simmer 5 minutes. Stir in butter; sprinkle croutons on top. *2 servings.*

GINGERBREAD STACKS WITH HOT BUTTERSCOTCH SAUCE

½ package (14.5-ounce size) gingerbread mix*
½ cup lukewarm water
¼ cup butterscotch ice-cream topping
   Vanilla ice cream

Heat oven to 350°. Grease and flour loaf pan, 9x5x3 inches. In small mixer bowl, mix gingerbread mix and lukewarm water on low speed. Beat on medium speed 2 minutes, scraping bowl frequently, or beat 300 strokes by hand. Pour into pan. Bake until wooden pick inserted in center comes out clean, 15 to 20 minutes.

Heat butterscotch topping. Cut 2 servings from gingerbread; split each piece. (Use remaining gingerbread as suggested below.) Fill layers with ice cream; top with hot butterscotch topping. *2 servings.*

* To use half the package, measure contents and divide in half (approximately 1½ cups). To store remaining mix, close package securely and use within 3 weeks to make hot gingerbread. Or make the entire package at one time and freeze leftover gingerbread for use as needed. Top it with applesauce and dash of cinnamon, whipped topping and sliced bananas, lemon sauce and cream cheese, vanilla ice cream and chocolate sauce or peach slices and mocha whipped cream.

Deep-dish Hamburger Pie
Cabbage Slaw (page 121)
Garlic Bun Sticks
Cherry-Berry Parfaits

DEEP-DISH HAMBURGER PIE

- ½ **pound ground beef**
- ¼ **cup chopped onion**
- ¼ **teaspoon salt**
- ⅛ **teaspoon pepper**
- ¼ **teaspoon monosodium glutamate**
- 1 **can (8 ounces) cut green beans, drained**
- ½ **can (10¾-ounce size) condensed tomato soup or**
  ½ cup catsup
- 1 **cup mashed potatoes**
- 3 **tablespoons shredded natural Cheddar cheese**

Heat oven to 350°. In 8-inch skillet, cook and stir meat and onion until meat is brown and onion is tender. Stir in seasonings, beans and soup. Pour into ungreased 1-quart casserole. Spoon mashed potatoes on mixture and top with cheese. Bake until mixture is hot and top is slightly brown, about 30 minutes. *2 servings.*

Note: Leftover mashed potatoes can be used in this recipe. Or prepare instant mashed potato puffs as directed on package for 2 servings.

GARLIC BUN STICKS

Heat oven to 350°. Brush soft butter or margarine on 1 split frankfurter bun or 2 slices bread. Sprinkle with garlic salt and cut into strips. Place on ungreased baking sheet. Bake until golden brown, about 15 minutes. *2 servings.*

CHERRY-BERRY PARFAITS

1 cup boiling water
1 package (3 ounces) cherry- or strawberry-flavored gelatin
1 package (10 ounces) frozen strawberries
¼ cup cold water

Pour boiling water on gelatin in bowl; stir until gelatin is dissolved. Stir in frozen strawberries until thawed. Stir in cold water. Chill until thickened but not set, about 1½ hours.

Pour 1½ cups of the gelatin mixture into bowl; beat until light and fluffy. (Use remaining gelatin mixture as suggested below.) Divide between parfait glasses or dessert dishes. Chill until set, about 1 hour. Garnish with a dollop of whipped topping. *2 servings.*

Note: You can use the remaining gelatin mixture for tomorrow's salad. Divide between 2 individual molds and chill until set. Or serve as a dessert if you like. Pour remaining gelatin mixture into small shallow container and chill until set. Cut gelatin into cubes and layer in parfait glasses with vanilla pudding or frozen whipped topping (thawed).

Italian Spaghetti
Tossed Spinach Salad
Butter Sticks
Biscuit Tortoni

ITALIAN SPAGHETTI

½ **pound ground beef**
3 **tablespoons minced onion**
1 **can (8 ounces) tomato sauce**
1 **can (6 ounces) tomato paste**
1 **cup water**
¼ **teaspoon salt**
¼ **teaspoon garlic powder**
¼ **teaspoon oregano leaves**
¼ **teaspoon basil**
3½ **to 4 ounces uncooked spaghetti**
    Grated Parmesan cheese

In 8-inch skillet, cook and stir meat until brown. Stir in remaining ingredients except spaghetti and cheese. Heat to boiling. Reduce heat; cover and simmer 1 hour. While sauce simmers, cook spaghetti as directed on package. Serve sauce on hot spaghetti; pass Parmesan cheese. *2 servings*.

TOSSED SPINACH SALAD

2 **cups bite-size pieces spinach leaves (about 5 ounces)**
2 **or 3 radishes, sliced**
2 **slices onion, separated into rings**
    Oil-and-vinegar dressing

Toss spinach, radish slices and onion rings in bowl. Serve salad with oil-and-vinegar dressing. *2 servings*.

BUTTER STICKS

¼ **cup butter or margarine**
1 **cup buttermilk baking mix**
¼ **cup water**
 Salt

Heat oven to 425°. In oven, melt butter in baking pan, 9x9x2 inches. Stir baking mix and water with fork to a soft dough. Turn onto floured cloth-covered board; smooth dough into ball and knead 5 times. Roll into rectangle, 6x4 inches. Cut into 8 strips, 4x¾ inch.

Dip each strip into melted butter, coating all sides, and arrange in pan. Sprinkle salt lightly on strips. Bake until golden brown, 10 to 12 minutes. *8 sticks.*

BISCUIT TORTONI

2 **tablespoons vanilla wafer or macaroon crumbs**
1 **tablespoon diced candied or well-drained maraschino**
 cherries
2 **tablespoons diced roasted almonds**
½ **pint vanilla ice cream (1 cup)**

Line 2 muffin cups with paper baking cups. Mix crumbs, cherries and almonds. Soften ice cream slightly; fold in crumb mixture. Divide ice-cream mixture between muffin cups. Decorate each with red cherry half and slices of green cherry to resemble a flower. Freeze until firm. *2 servings.*

Garlic-Chip Chicken
Quick Scalloped Potatoes
Skillet Asparagus
Cranberry Relish Salad
Brownies à la Mode

GARLIC-CHIP CHICKEN

¼ **cup shortening (part butter) or salad oil**
1 **teaspoon garlic salt**
⅛ **teaspoon pepper**
1½ **pounds chicken pieces or 2-pound broiler-fryer
    chicken, quartered**
1 **bag (3½ ounces) potato chips, crushed (about 1½
    cups)**

Heat oven to 400°. In oven, melt shortening with garlic
salt and pepper in baking pan, 9x9x2 inches. Dip
chicken into shortening to coat all sides, then roll in
potato chips. Place skin side down in pan. Bake uncovered 30 minutes. Turn; bake until thickest pieces
are tender, about 30 minutes. *2 servings*.

QUICK SCALLOPED POTATOES

Heat oven to 400°. Measure contents of 1 package
(5.5 ounces) scalloped potatoes; divide in half (approximately 1 cup potato slices and 3 tablespoons sauce
mix).* Place half the potato slices in ungreased 2½-
cup or 1-quart casserole. Sprinkle 3 tablespoons sauce
mix on slices. Stir in half the amounts of butter, water
and milk called for on package. Bake uncovered until
potatoes are tender and golden brown, 25 to 30 minutes. *2 generous servings*.

* To store remaining mix, close package securely and
use within 2 weeks to make Scalloped Potatoes with
Ham (page 155) or Hot Potato Salad (page 15).

SKILLET ASPARAGUS

Break off tough ends of ¾ to 1 pound asparagus as far down as stalks snap easily. Wash asparagus and remove scales if sandy or tough. Fill 10-inch skillet ⅓ full with water; add ½ teaspoon salt and heat to boiling. Add asparagus; heat to boiling. Cover and cook until stalk ends are crisp-tender, 8 to 12 minutes. Drain; return asparagus to skillet to dry. Dot with 1 tablespoon butter or margarine. *2 servings.*

CRANBERRY RELISH SALAD

1 cup boiling water
1 package (3 ounces) lemon-flavored gelatin
1 package (10 ounces) frozen cranberry-orange relish
   Lettuce

Pour boiling water onto gelatin in bowl; stir until gelatin is dissolved. Stir in frozen relish until thawed. Pour into 4-cup mold or 4 to 6 individual molds. Chill until firm. Place 2 servings on lettuce; if desired, top with mayonnaise. Serve remaining gelatin topped with whipped cream as dessert the next day. *2 servings— and 2 more for another day.*

Note: Pineapple-flavored gelatin can be substituted for the lemon-flavored gelatin. And for variety, add one of the following: 1 can (8¾ ounces) crushed pineapple (with syrup); 1 apple, chopped; ⅓ cup chopped nuts.

BROWNIES À LA MODE

Bake Brownies (page 80) or 1 package (15.5 ounces) fudge brownie mix as directed. For each serving, place scoop of vanilla, coffee or peppermint ice cream on brownie square. Heat ¼ cup chocolate fudge sauce; drizzle on ice cream.

Salmon Piquant
Potato Puffs
Stewed Tomatoes
Crisp Relishes
Easy Blueberry Tarts

SALMON PIQUANT

- **1 package (12 ounces) frozen salmon steaks**
- **¼ cup tartar sauce**
- **½ cup canned French fried onions***

Heat oven to 450°. Place frozen fish in ungreased shallow baking dish. Bake uncovered until fish flakes easily with fork, 15 to 20 minutes. Spread tartar sauce on fish; sprinkle onions on top. Bake until sauce is hot and onions are crisp, 2 to 3 minutes. *2 servings.*

Variation

Halibut Piquant: Substitute 1 package (12 ounces) frozen halibut steaks for the salmon.

* Extra French fried onions? Sprinkle on a tossed green salad or add as a crunchy topping for hot cooked asparagus, green beans, broccoli or other vegetables.

POTATO PUFFS

Heat oven to 450°. On ungreased baking sheet, spread ½ package (16-ounce size) frozen fried shredded potato rounds. Bake until hot and crisp, about 15 minutes. *2 servings.*

EASY BLUEBERRY TARTS

Bake Tart Shells (below) or use commercially prepared tart shells. Fill 2 shells with ½ can (21-ounce size) blueberry pie filling or your favorite pie filling (cherry, peach, lemon, strawberry). Top each with dollop of whipped topping or dairy sour cream. Garnish with grated lemon peel or sprinkle of cinnamon. *2 servings*.

Tart Shells

Heat oven to 450°. Prepare pastry for One-crust Pie as directed on 1 package (11 ounces) pie crust mix or sticks except—divide dough into 6 equal parts. Roll each part into 4-inch circle. Fit circles into individual pie pans or tart pans. Or fit over backs of muffin cups or 6-ounce custard cups, making pleats so pastry will fit closely. Prick with fork and place on baking sheet. Bake 8 to 10 minutes. Cool and remove from pans. *6 tart shells*.

Note: Unfilled tart shells can be frozen for future use.

SOMETHING TO KNOW ABOUT...

To make Tart Shells if you don't have tart pans, alternate circles of pastry over the backs of muffin cups, pleating them to insure a snug fit. Prick them with a fork; make sure not to forget to do the sides. The baked Tart Shells can be filled with almost anything: Think in terms of pudding, ice cream, canned pie filling, fruit—the possibilities are endless.

Mustard Short Ribs
Baked Sweet Potatoes
Italian Green Beans
Apple-Celery Toss or Cabbage Slaw
Butterscotch Bread Pudding

MUSTARD SHORT RIBS

2 pounds beef short ribs, cut into pieces
2 medium onions, sliced
2 tablespoons prepared mustard
1 tablespoon lemon juice
1 teaspoon sugar
1 teaspoon salt
½ teaspoon instant minced garlic
½ teaspoon pepper

Heat oven to 350°. In 8-inch skillet, brown meat over medium heat. Place meat and onion slices in ungreased 2-quart casserole. Mix remaining ingredients; pour on meat. Cover tightly and bake until meat is tender, about 1½ hours. *2 servings.*

BAKED SWEET POTATOES

Heat oven to 350°. Rub 2 medium sweet potatoes with shortening (for soft skins). Prick with fork to allow steam to escape. Bake until tender, about 1 hour.

To serve, cut crisscross gash in each top; squeeze gently until some of potato pops up through opening. Serve with butter or dairy sour cream. *2 servings.*

APPLE-CELERY TOSS

1½ **cups bite-size pieces lettuce**
1 **red apple, sliced**
¼ **cup diagonally sliced celery**
¼ **cup mayonnaise or oil-and-vinegar dressing**

Combine lettuce, apple slices and celery in bowl. Pour mayonnaise on and toss. *2 servings.*

CABBAGE SLAW

2 **cups coarsely shredded cabbage (about ⅓ head)**
¼ **cup coarsely chopped unpared cucumber**
Dash salt
¼ **cup mayonnaise or salad dressing**

Combine cabbage, cucumber and salt in bowl. Pour mayonnaise on cabbage mixture and toss. *2 servings.*

BUTTERSCOTCH BREAD PUDDING

1 **cup soft bread cubes**
1 **egg**
1 **tablespoon butter or margarine, melted**
⅔ **cup milk**
3 **tablespoons brown sugar**
½ **teaspoon cinnamon**
¼ **teaspoon nutmeg**
Dash salt
⅓ **cup raisins**

Heat oven to 350°. Place bread cubes in buttered 2½-cup casserole. Beat egg slightly; stir in butter, milk, brown sugar, seasonings and raisins. Pour egg mixture on bread cubes. Bake until knife inserted halfway between center and edge comes out clean, about 40 minutes. Serve warm. Top with light cream if you like. *2 servings.*

Pot Roast with Carrots and Onions
Herbed Noodles
Tossed Green Salad
Whole Wheat Rolls
Warm Caramel Pears

POT ROAST WITH CARROTS AND ONIONS

2 tablespoons salad oil
2- pound beef chuck pot roast
½ teaspoon salt
¼ teaspoon pepper
½ cup water
4 medium carrots, halved lengthwise
4 small onions
¼ teaspoon salt
Kettle Gravy (below), if desired

Heat oil in Dutch oven or large skillet; brown meat over medium heat, about 15 minutes. Sprinkle ½ teaspoon salt and the pepper on meat. Add water; cover tightly and simmer on range or in 325° oven 1½ hours. (Add small amount of water if necessary.) Add vegetables and ¼ teaspoon salt; cook until meat is tender and vegetables are done, about ½ hour.

Place meat and vegetables on warm platter; keep warm while making gravy. Serve meat with gravy. *2 servings.*

Kettle Gravy

Skim excess fat from meat broth. Measure broth; if necessary add enough water (or vegetable cooking liquid, consommé or vegetable juice) to measure ½ cup and pour into pan. Mix 2 tablespoons cold water and 1 tablespoon flour. Stir flour mixture into broth. Heat to boiling, stirring constantly. Boil and stir 1 minute. If desired, stir in few drops bottled brown bouquet sauce. Season with salt and pepper. If you prefer a thinner gravy, stir in small amount of additional liquid. *½ cup.*

Note: If using quick-mixing flour, just stir into cold water with fork. If using regular flour, shake water and flour in covered jar—be sure to put water in jar first, then the flour.

HERBED NOODLES

   3 **to 4 ounces uncooked noodles (1 to 1½ cups)**
¼ **teaspoon thyme leaves**
¼ **teaspoon basil leaves**
¼ **teaspoon snipped parsley**
¼ **teaspoon snipped chives or finely chopped onion**
   1 **tablespoon butter or margarine, melted**

Cook noodles in 1 quart boiling salted water (1½ teaspoons salt) until tender, 7 to 10 minutes. Drain noodles and return to saucepan. Mix remaining ingredients; pour onto noodles and toss. *2 servings.*

WARM CARAMEL PEARS

   1 **can (8 ounces) pear halves**
      Vanilla ice cream
¼ **teaspoon cinnamon**
¼ **cup caramel ice-cream topping**

Heat pears (with syrup) in small saucepan. Drain. Spoon pears into serving dishes. Top with scoops of ice cream. Stir cinnamon into caramel topping; pour on each serving. *2 servings.*

SOMETHING TO KNOW ABOUT ...

To insure that Kettle Gravy will be smooth, stir constantly as you add the flour-water to the broth. The broth will have more flavor and color if the meat was browned slowly.

Frankfurters
Hot German Potato Salad
Buttered Green Beans
Cherry Skillet Cobbler

FRANKFURTERS

Drop 4 large frankfurters (about ¾ pound) into boiling water. Cover; reduce heat and simmer until heated through, 5 to 8 minutes. Remove frankfurters from water with tongs. *2 servings.*

HOT GERMAN POTATO SALAD

 2 **medium potatoes, pared and halved**
 3 **slices bacon**
⅓ **cup chopped onion**
 1 **tablespoon flour**
 2 **teaspoons sugar**
¾ **teaspoon salt**
¼ **teaspoon celery seed**
    Dash pepper
⅓ **cup water**
 3 **tablespoons vinegar**

Heat 1 inch salted water (½ teaspoon salt to 1 cup water) to boiling. Add potatoes. Cover and heat to boiling; cook until tender, 20 to 25 minutes. Drain and set aside.

In 8-inch skillet, fry bacon until crisp; remove and drain. In same skillet, cook and stir onion in bacon fat until tender. Stir in flour, sugar, salt, celery seed and pepper. Cook over low heat, stirring until mixture is bubbly. Remove from heat. Stir in water and vinegar.

Heat to boiling, stirring constantly. Boil and stir 1 minute. Remove from heat.

Crumble bacon into hot mixture, then slice warm potatoes into hot mixture. Cook until hot and bubbly, stirring lightly to coat potato slices. *2 servings.*

BUTTERED GREEN BEANS

Cook ½ package (9-ounce size) frozen cut green beans as directed except—use only half the amounts of water and salt called for on package. Drain. Dot with 1 tablespoon butter or margarine and sprinkle with chopped salted peanuts, sunflower seeds or almonds. *2 servings.*

CHERRY SKILLET COBBLER

   ½ can (21-ounce size) cherry pie filling
   ¼ cup orange juice
   ½ cup buttermilk baking mix
   1 tablespoon shredded orange peel, if desired
 1½ teaspoons sugar
   2 tablespoons milk

In 1-quart saucepan, heat pie filling and orange juice to boiling, stirring occasionally. Stir baking mix, orange peel, sugar and milk with fork to a soft dough. Drop dough by spoonfuls (2 or 3) onto boiling cherry mixture. Cook uncovered over low heat 10 minutes; cover and cook 10 minutes longer. Serve warm. Top with light cream or ice cream if you wish. *2 servings.*

Liver Italiano
Spaghetti
Green Bean Tossed Salad
Lime Frappé
Vanilla Wafers

LIVER ITALIANO

2 tablespoons flour
½ teaspoon garlic salt
½ pound sliced beef liver, cut into 1-inch pieces
1 tablespoon salad oil
1 can (8 ounces) tomato sauce
1 green pepper, cut into thin strips
1 small onion, thinly sliced and separated into rings
3 to 4 ounces uncooked spaghetti
2 tablespoons grated Parmesan cheese

Mix flour and garlic salt; coat meat with flour mixture. Heat oil in 8-inch skillet; brown meat over medium heat. Stir in tomato sauce; add green pepper and onion. Cover and simmer until done, 8 to 10 minutes.

While meat simmers, cook spaghetti as directed on package. Serve meat mixture on spaghetti and sprinkle cheese on top. *2 servings.*

GREEN BEAN TOSSED SALAD

1 can (8 ounces) cut green beans, chilled
1 can (2 ounces) mushroom stems and pieces, chilled
1 cup bite-size pieces lettuce
1 teaspoon chopped pimiento
3 tablespoons Italian dressing
2 lettuce cups

Drain green beans and mushrooms. Toss beans, mushrooms, lettuce, pimiento and dressing in bowl. Divide salad between lettuce cups. *2 servings.*

LIME FRAPPÉ

2 **cups crushed ice**
½ **can (6-ounce size) frozen limeade concentrate
(about ¼ cup)***
2 **tablespoons sugar**
1 **drop green food color**

In blender, mix all ingredients on medium speed until mixture is consistency of sherbet. (Scrape sides once or twice if necessary.) Serve immediately or store in freezer until serving time. *2 servings.*

Note: To crush ice, use an ice crusher or wrap 9 or 10 ice cubes in towel and crush with mallet or hammer.

* Leftover limeade concentrate? To the rescue for tomorrow's dessert: Top servings of cut-up fresh or canned fruit with spoonfuls of the partially thawed concentrate.

SOMETHING TO KNOW ABOUT . . .

"Liver's good for you!" Sound familiar? Well, it's no old wives' tale. Liver is positively packed with essential nutrients, including protein, iron, vitamin A, riboflavin and niacin. It's a good idea to work it into your meal plan every week or two. But liver is more perishable than other meats; unless it's frozen, it should be used within 2 days after purchase.

Beef and pork livers are frequently braised or fried and are sometimes ground for loaves and patties. Baby beef, veal (calf) and lamb liver are usually panfried, broiled or panbroiled. Before cooking, peel or trim any membrane from the liver if necessary. If you simply can't take it "straight," try grinding it up as part of your meat loaf mixture or use it as a sandwich spread.

Chili con Carne
Cucumber-Iceberg Salad
Ripe Olives
Cornmeal Butter Sticks
Pineapple Pudding

CHILI CON CARNE

½ pound ground beef
1 medium onion, chopped (about ½ cup)
½ cup chopped green pepper
1 can (16 ounces) tomatoes
1 can (8 ounces) tomato sauce
1 teaspoon salt
1 to 2 teaspoons chili powder
  Dash cayenne red pepper
  Dash paprika
1 can (8 ounces) kidney beans

In 8-inch skillet, cook and stir meat, onion and green pepper until meat is brown and onion is tender. Drain off fat. Stir in remaining ingredients except beans. Heat to boiling. Reduce heat; cook uncovered about 30 minutes. Stir in beans (with liquid); heat until bubbly. *2 servings.*

CUCUMBER-ICEBERG SALAD

1½ cups shredded iceberg lettuce
 ½ medium cucumber, cut into cubes
  Grated Parmesan cheese
  Oil-and-vinegar dressing

Toss lettuce and cucumber cubes in bowl; sprinkle cheese on top. Serve with dressing. *2 servings.*

CORNMEAL BUTTER STICKS

¼ **cup butter or margarine**
½ **cup buttermilk baking mix**
½ **cup cornmeal**
¼ **cup water**
    Salt

Heat oven to 450°. In oven, melt butter in baking pan, 9x9x2 inches. Stir baking mix, cornmeal and water with fork to soft dough. Turn onto floured cloth-covered board; smooth dough into ball and knead 5 times. Roll into rectangle, 6x4 inches. Cut into 8 strips, 4x¾ inch.

Dip each strip into melted butter, coating all sides, and arrange in pan. Sprinkle salt lightly on strips. Bake until golden brown, 12 to 15 minutes. Serve hot. *8 sticks.*

PINEAPPLE PUDDING

 1 **can (8½ ounces) crushed pineapple, drained**
½ **can (18-ounce size) vanilla pudding (1 cup)**
    Toasted coconut

Fold pineapple into pudding; divide between dessert dishes. Chill. Top each serving with coconut. *2 servings.*

> **Chicken Cacciatore**
> **Spaghetti**
> **Zucchini Parmesan**
> **Fresh Spinach Salad**
> **Rainbow Parfaits**

CHICKEN CACCIATORE

     Salad oil
 ¼ cup all-purpose flour
 ½ teaspoon salt
 ⅛ teaspoon pepper
 ⅛ teaspoon paprika
 1 to 1½ pounds chicken pieces or 2-pound
     broiler-fryer chicken, cut up
 1 jar (15 ounces) meatless spaghetti sauce
 1 can (2 ounces) mushroom stems and pieces
 ¼ teaspoon instant minced garlic
 1 teaspoon parsley flakes
 ¼ cup sliced pitted ripe olives
3½ to 4 ounces uncooked spaghetti

Heat ⅛ inch salad oil in large skillet. Mix flour, salt,
pepper and paprika; coat chicken with flour mixture.
Cook chicken in oil over medium heat until light brown,
15 to 20 minutes. Mix spaghetti sauce, mushrooms
(with liquid), garlic, parsley flakes and olives. Drain
fat from skillet. Pour sauce onto chicken. Heat to boiling. Reduce heat; cover tightly and simmer until thickest pieces of chicken are tender, about 30 minutes.

   While chicken simmers, cook spaghetti as directed on
package. Drain. Serve chicken with spaghetti. *2 servings.*

ZUCCHINI PARMESAN

Cut 1 medium zucchini into strips, 2x½ inch. Heat 1 inch salted water (½ teaspoon salt to 1 cup water) to boiling. Add zucchini. Cover and heat to boiling; cook until tender, 7 to 9 minutes. Drain. Add 1 tablespoon butter or margarine and toss. Sprinkle 1 tablespoon grated Parmesan cheese on zucchini. *2 servings.*

FRESH SPINACH SALAD

2 cups bite-size pieces spinach leaves (about 5 ounces)
2 green onions, sliced
  Seasoned salt
2 tablespoons bacon-flavored vegetable protein chips
2 tablespoons oil-and-vinegar dressing

Divide spinach between salad bowls. Sprinkle onion slices, seasoned salt and vegetable protein chips on spinach. Drizzle 1 tablespoon dressing on each serving. If you like, garnish with lemon twists. *2 servings.*

RAINBOW PARFAITS

Choose 2 or 3 flavors sherbet, such as raspberry, pineapple and/or lime (about ½ pint each). Make balls with scoop or spoon. Divide between parfait glasses and place in freezer.

At serving time, fill glasses with ginger ale, and if desired, garnish each with whipped topping. *2 servings.*

BONUS MAIN DISHES

ORIENTAL GLAZED CHICKEN

1½ **pounds chicken pieces or 2-pound broiler-fryer chicken, quartered**
⅓ **cup soy sauce**
2 **tablespoons salad oil**
2 **tablespoons chili sauce**
¼ **cup honey**
1 **teaspoon salt**
½ **teaspoon ginger**
¼ **teaspoon garlic powder**
¼ **teaspoon cayenne red pepper, if desired**

Place chicken in baking pan, 9x9x2 inches. Mix remaining ingredients; pour on chicken. Cover and refrigerate at least 1 hour, turning chicken occasionally.

Heat oven to 375°. Remove chicken; reserve marinade. Place chicken on rack in foil-lined broiler pan. Bake 30 minutes; brush with part of reserved marinade. Turn chicken; bake until tender, about 30 minutes longer, brushing occasionally with remaining marinade. *2 servings.*

Play up the Oriental theme with hot cooked rice, Mixed Vegetable Salad (page 74) and lemon sherbet with Quick Date Cake (page 58).

SPICED CHICKEN WITH FRUIT

2 **tablespoons salad oil**
¾ **teaspoon salt**
¼ **teaspoon cayenne red pepper**
1½ **pounds chicken pieces or 2-pound broiler-fryer chicken, cut up**
½ **cup pineapple chunks**
⅓ **cup raisins**
½ **cup pineapple juice or orange juice**
⅛ **teaspoon cinnamon**
⅛ **teaspoon cloves**
  Orange sections
  Parsley

Heat oil in large skillet. Mix salt and cayenne red pepper; sprinkle on chicken. Cook chicken in oil over medium heat until light brown, 15 to 20 minutes. Add remaining ingredients except orange sections and parsley. Reduce heat; cover tightly and simmer until thickest pieces are tender, 20 to 25 minutes. Garnish with orange sections and parsley. *2 servings.*

Round out this zingy meal with hot cooked rice, Tossed Spinach Salad (page 114) and Butterscotch Cake Sundaes (page 25).

BROILED CHILI CHICKEN

1½ pounds chicken pieces or 2-pound broiler-fryer chicken, halved or quartered
¼ cup butter or margarine, melted
2 tablespoons white wine vinegar
2 teaspoons chili powder
1 teaspoon salt

Set oven control at broil and/or 550°. Place chicken skin side down on rack in broiler pan. Mix butter, vinegar, chili powder and salt; brush part of mixture on chicken.

Broil chicken with top 7 to 9 inches* from heat, basting occasionally with butter-chili mixture, about 30 minutes. Turn chicken; broil until tender, 20 to 30 minutes, basting occasionally with remaining mixture. *2 servings.*

Cool go-alongs with this spicy chicken: shoestring potatoes, Green Bean Tossed Salad (page 127) and Frosty Pumpkin Custards (page 61).

* If it is not possible to place the broiler pan this far from the heat source, reduce temperature to 450°.

CRUNCHY BAKED DRUMSTICKS

1 pound chicken drumsticks
Salt and pepper
¼ cup butter or margarine, melted
½ cup crushed corn flake cereal

Heat oven to 350°. Sprinkle chicken with salt and pepper. Dip into butter, then roll in cereal. Place in greased baking pan, 8x8x2 inches. Drizzle remaining butter on chicken. Bake uncovered until tender, about 1 hour. *2 servings.*

Try these chilled for a picnic. Serve with Fresh Vegetables Vinaigrette (page 67), buttered French bread, Brownies (page 80) and a thermos of iced tea or coffee.

CHICKEN ITALIAN IN FOIL

For each serving:

    Salad oil
 2 meaty chicken pieces (thigh, leg or breast)
¼ teaspoon salt
 1 medium potato, pared
 1 medium zucchini
 3 large pitted ripe olives
 2 tablespoons catsup
½ teaspoon oregano leaves
 1 tablespoon butter or margarine
    Grated Parmesan cheese, if desired

Heat oven to 400°. Brush oil on chicken pieces; sprinkle with ¼ teaspoon salt. Cut potato lengthwise into ⅛-inch slices. Place potato slices on 18x12-inch piece of double thickness heavy-duty aluminum foil; sprinkle with salt. Cut unpared zucchini into ¼-inch slices. Place zucchini on potato; sprinkle with salt. Place chicken pieces and olives on zucchini; top with catsup, oregano and butter. Wrap securely in foil. Bake until chicken and vegetables are tender, about 1 hour. Sprinkle with Parmesan cheese.

Tasty and easy when served with Tossed Romaine Salad (page 195), crusty rolls and green grapes.

To Grill: Cook on grill 5 inches from medium coals 25 to 30 minutes on each side.

HAMBURGER AU GRATIN SKILLET

½ pound ground beef
½ package (5.5-ounce size) au gratin potatoes*
¼ teaspoon salt

In 8-inch skillet, cook and stir meat until brown. Drain off fat. Add potato slices and salt to meat. Sprinkle sauce mix on top. Stir in half the amounts of water and milk called for on package. Heat to boiling, stirring occasionally. Reduce heat; cover and simmer, stirring occasionally, until potatoes are tender, about 30 minutes. *2 servings.*

* To use half the package, measure contents and divide in half (approximately 1 cup potato slices and 3 tablespoons sauce mix). To store remaining mix, close package securely; use within 2 weeks. Make Canadian Cheese Soup (page 84) or Quick au Gratin Potatoes (page 19).

Variation

Potatoes Stroganoff: Substitute garlic salt for the salt; after simmering, stir in 1 can (2 ounces) mushroom stems and pieces (with liquid) and ¼ cup dairy sour cream and heat through.

Serve with buttered peas, Herbed Tomatoes (page 7) and chocolate ice cream.

SALISBURY STEAK WITH MUSHROOM SAUCE

½ **pound ground beef**
½ **teaspoon salt**
⅛ **teaspoon pepper**
1 **can (2 ounces) sliced mushrooms, drained
(reserve liquid)**
1 **tablespoon flour**
1 **teaspoon instant beef bouillon or 1 beef bouillon cube**

Mix meat, salt and pepper; shape mixture into 2 oval patties. In 8-inch skillet, cook patties over medium heat, turning occasionally, until done, 8 to 12 minutes. Remove patties to warm plate.

Cook and stir mushrooms in same skillet until light brown. Stir in flour. Cook over low heat, stirring until mixture is bubbly. Remove from heat. Add enough water to reserved mushroom liquid to measure ½ cup. Stir liquid and bouillon into flour mixture. Heat to boiling, stirring constantly. Boil and stir 1 minute. Pour on meat. *2 servings.*

We suggest these classic accompaniments: mashed

potatoes, green peas, Orange-Cucumber Salad (page 95) and Praline Squares (page 44).

HAMBURGERS

½ **pound ground beef**
 1 **tablespoon chopped onion or 1 teaspoon instant minced onion**
½ **teaspoon salt**
⅛ **teaspoon pepper**

Mix all ingredients. Shape into 2 patties, each about 3 inches in diameter and 1 inch thick.

To Broil: Set oven control at broil and/or 550°. Broil with tops 3 inches from heat 3 to 4 minutes on each side for rare, 5 to 7 minutes on each side for medium.

To Panfry: Melt 1 to 2 teaspoons shortening in 8-inch skillet; cook patties over medium heat, turning frequently, until done, about 10 minutes.

To Bake: Place on rack in baking pan; bake in 350° oven 20 to 25 minutes for rare, 30 minutes for medium. *2 servings.*

Variations

Horseradish Burgers: Add 1½ teaspoons horseradish before mixing ingredients.

Mustard and Pickle Burgers: Add 1½ teaspoons dry mustard and 1 tablespoon pickle relish before mixing ingredients.

Cheeseburgers: About 1 minute before hamburgers are done, top each patty with cheese slice; continue cooking until cheese is melted.

California Hamburgers: Top each cooked patty with lettuce, onion slice, tomato slice and dab of mayonnaise.

Barbecued Hamburgers: Mix 2 tablespoons catsup, 1 tablespoon brown sugar, ½ teaspoon dry mustard and ⅛ teaspoon nutmeg. Brush mixture on patties before and after turning.

To perk up these appetite-pleasers, serve with coleslaw, potato chips, chilled apricots and Quick Date Cake (page 58).

VIENNESE STEAK

¾- pound beef round steak, ½ to ¾ inch thick
2 tablespoons shortening
¼ cup water
½ teaspoon salt
¼ teaspoon pepper
2 medium onions, thinly sliced
1 can (10½ ounces) condensed cream of mushroom
  soup
  Snipped parsley

Cut meat into 2 pieces. Melt shortening in 8-inch skillet; brown meat over medium heat, about 15 minutes. Add water; sprinkle with salt and pepper and top with onions.

Reduce heat; cover and simmer until tender, about 1 hour. (Add small amount of water if necessary.) Remove meat to warm platter; keep warm.

Drain off fat from skillet. Stir in soup and heat; pour on meat and garnish with parsley. *2 servings*.

This attractive dish is well teamed with hot cooked noodles or mashed potatoes, buttered beets, Orange-Cucumber Salad (page 95) and Butterscotch Cake Sundaes (page 25).

TEXAS HASH

½ pound ground beef
2 medium onions, sliced
1 small green pepper, chopped
1 can (8 ounces) stewed tomatoes
¼ cup uncooked regular rice
½ to 1 teaspoon chili powder
1 teaspoon salt

Heat oven to 350°. In 8-inch skillet, cook and stir meat, onion and green pepper until meat is brown and vegetables are tender. Drain off fat. Stir in remaining ingredients; heat through. Pour into ungreased 1-quart casserole. Cover and bake until rice is tender, 30 to 35 minutes. *2 servings*.

Suggested accompaniments: vegetable relishes, fruit salad and Brownies (page 80).

MACARONI-BEEF SAUTÉ

½ **pound ground beef**
2 **ounces uncooked elbow macaroni (½ cup)**
1 **small onion, chopped**
¼ **cup chopped green pepper**
2 **tablespoons salad oil**
1 **can (12 ounces) tomato juice**
½ **teaspoon garlic salt**
½ **teaspoon salt**
⅛ **teaspoon pepper**
1 **teaspoon Worcestershire sauce**

In medium skillet, cook and stir meat, macaroni, onion and green pepper in oil until meat is brown and macaroni is light yellow. Drain off fat. Stir in remaining ingredients; heat to boiling. Reduce heat; cover and simmer until macaroni is tender, about 20 minutes. Uncover and simmer until sauce is desired consistency. *2 generous servings.*

Great with green beans, Cucumber-Iceberg Salad (page 128) and pineapple sherbet.

BRAISED LAMB SHANKS AND VEGETABLES

1 **tablespoon salad oil**
2 **lamb shanks**
½ **cup water**
1 **tablespoon lemon juice**
½ **teaspoon salt**
½ **teaspoon rosemary leaves**
⅛ **teaspoon lemon pepper**
1 **small clove garlic, crushed, or ⅛ teaspoon garlic powder**
1 **bay leaf**
4 **small onions**
4 **or 5 small carrots, cut into halves**
2 **medium potatoes, pared and cut into halves**
1 **package (10 ounces) frozen Italian green beans, broken apart**
½ **teaspoon salt**

Heat oil in Dutch oven; brown meat. Add water, lemon juice, ½ teaspoon salt, the rosemary leaves, pepper, garlic and bay leaf. Cover tightly and simmer on range or in 350° oven 1 hour. (Add small amount of water if necessary.) Add vegetables and ½ teaspoon salt; cook until meat and vegetables are tender, 40 to 60 minutes. *2 servings.*

Note: You can substitute 1 can (16 ounces) whole green beans, drained, for the Italian green beans. Add during the last 5 to 10 minutes of cooking.

A carefree meal-in-one that needs only crisp lettuce wedges and a favorite dressing. For dessert, serve Velvet Crumb Cake with Pineapple Sauce (page 106).

PLANNING
AHEAD

**Dinners that star a "big" meat buy—
with repeat performances as sparkling as First Night**

Mint-glazed Roast Lamb
Bulgur Pilaf
Spinach Soufflé (page 199)
Greek Salad (page 183)
Gourmet Pears

MINT-GLAZED ROAST LAMB

Place roast fat side up on rack in shallow roasting pan. Season with salt and pepper before, during or after roasting (salt goes into roast only ¼ to ½ inch). Insert meat thermometer so tip is in thickest part of meat and does not touch bone or rest in fat.

Roast uncovered in 325° oven to desired doneness (see Timetable), using thermometer reading as final guide. During last hour of roasting, brush meat every 15 minutes with Mint Glaze (below). Serve any remaining glaze with roast.

Roasts are easier to carve if allowed to "set" 15 to 20 minutes after removing from oven. Since meat continues to cook after removal from oven, if roast is to set, it should be removed from oven when thermometer registers 5 to 10° lower than the desired doneness.

Mint Glaze

Heat ½ jar (10-ounce size) mint-flavored jelly, 1 clove garlic, crushed, and 2 teaspoons water, stirring constantly, until jelly is melted.

TIMETABLE

Cut	Approximate Cooking Time (Minutes per Lb.)	Meat Thermometer Reading
Rolled Leg		
3 to 5 lbs.	35 to 40	175 to 180°
Leg		
5 to 6 lbs.	30 to 35	175 to 180°
Square Shoulder		
4 to 6 lbs.	30 to 35	175 to 180°

BULGUR PILAF

1 tablespoon finely chopped onion
1 tablespoon chopped green pepper
1 tablespoon butter or margarine
⅔ cup hot water
½ teaspoon instant chicken bouillon
⅓ cup bulgur wheat
1 can (2 ounces) sliced mushrooms, drained
¼ teaspoon salt
Dash pepper

In 8-inch skillet, cook and stir onion and green pepper in butter until onion is tender. Stir in remaining ingredients. Heat to boiling. Reduce heat; cover and simmer 10 minutes. *2 servings.*

GOURMET PEARS

1 egg yolk*
3 tablespoons dairy sour cream
3 tablespoons granulated sugar
1 tablespoon rum, brandy or sherry
1 can (8 ounces) pears, drained
2 tablespoons brown sugar

In small saucepan, mix egg yolk, sour cream and granulated sugar. Cook, stirring constantly, until sauce is thickened, about 3 minutes. Cool. (Store in refrigerator if not using immediately.)

Stir rum into sour cream sauce. Place pears in 2 ungreased 6-ounce baking dishes or one 1¾-cup casserole. Pour sauce onto pears; sprinkle with brown sugar. Set oven control at broil and/or 550°. Broil with tops 6 to 8 inches from heat until brown sugar melts, 3 to 4 minutes. Serve hot or chilled. *2 servings.*

* What about the egg white? Store in covered small container in refrigerator up to 3 days. Can be used for Individual Brownie Alaskas (page 7) or Meringue Shells (page 189)—fill shells with ice cream.

Look-ahead lamb still has that international air. When the next time comes, go East or West— Chinese or American.

CHOPPED LAMB SANDWICH FILLING

- ½ cup chopped cooked lamb
- 2 tablespoons mayonnaise or salad dressing
- 3 tablespoons finely chopped celery
- 1½ teaspoons finely chopped onion
- 1 teaspoon prepared mustard

Mix all ingredients. Good on rye bread. *¾ cup (enough for 2 sandwiches).*

CHINESE LAMB SUEY

- 2 tablespoons butter or margarine
- 1½ cups cooked lamb strips, 2 x ¼ x ¼ inch
- 1 small onion, sliced and separated into rings
- ½ can (8-ounce size) water chestnuts, sliced*
- ¾ cup water
- 1 tablespoon soy sauce
- 1 tablespoon cornstarch
- ¾ teaspoon instant beef bouillon
- ½ teaspoon salt
- 1 package (6 ounces) frozen pea pods
  Hot cooked rice or chow mein noodles

Melt butter in 8-inch skillet; cook and stir meat and onion over medium heat until meat is brown and onion is tender. Add remaining ingredients except pea pods and rice. Heat to boiling, stirring occasionally. Add pea pods; cover and simmer 5 minutes. Serve on rice. *2 servings.*

* Leftover water chestnuts? Slice and add to a crisp

salad or cooked vegetable. Or use in Scallops en Brochette (page 176).

SHEPHERDS' PIE

Instant mashed potato puffs (enough for 4 servings)
1 tablespoon parsley flakes or snipped parsley
1 envelope (about 1 ounce) gravy mix
1 cup cubed cooked lamb, beef or veal
2 tablespoons chopped onion
1 cup cooked vegetables (peas, carrots, corn,
  green beans)
¼ teaspoon salt

Heat oven to 350°. Prepare potato puffs as directed on package except—stir in parsley flakes. Prepare gravy mix as directed.

In ungreased 1-quart casserole, mix gravy and remaining ingredients. Mound potatoes on meat mixture. Bake uncovered until potatoes are light brown, 25 to 30 minutes. *2 servings*.

LAMB WITH DILL SAUCE

1 tablespoon butter or margarine
1 tablespoon flour
⅓ cup water
½ teaspoon instant chicken bouillon
2 tablespoons vinegar
½ teaspoon dill weed
  Salt and pepper
2 to 4 slices cooked lamb, ⅜ inch thick

Melt butter in small saucepan. Stir in flour. Cook over low heat, stirring until mixture is smooth and bubbly. Stir in water and bouillon. Heat to boiling, stirring constantly. Boil and stir 1 minute. Stir in vinegar and dill weed. Season with salt and pepper. Add meat and heat. Garnish with snipped parsley if desired. *2 servings*.

Corned Beef and Cabbage with Horseradish Sauce
Anadama Batter Bread
Creamy Peach Pudding or Quick Mocha Dessert
or Ginger Cookies (see below)

CORNED BEEF AND CABBAGE

2- to 3-pound beef corned brisket
2 small onions
4 small carrots
2 small potatoes, pared and halved
½ green cabbage, cut into wedges
Horseradish Sauce (below)

Cook meat as directed on package. If directions are not available, place meat in Dutch oven; cover with hot water. Heat to boiling. Reduce heat; cover tightly and simmer until tender, 3 to 3½ hours.

About 20 minutes before meat is tender, skim fat from liquid, then add onions, carrots and potatoes. Cover and simmer 20 minutes. Remove meat and keep warm.

Add cabbage to liquid; simmer uncovered until vegetables are tender, 10 to 15 minutes. To carve meat, cut thin diagonal slices across the grain. Serve with Horseradish Sauce. *2 servings.*

Horseradish Sauce

⅓ cup mayonnaise or dairy sour cream
1 tablespoon horseradish
Dash paprika
Dash dry mustard

Mix all ingredients. Refrigerate until serving time. *About ⅓ cup.*

ANADAMA BATTER BREAD

¾ **cup boiling water**
½ **cup yellow cornmeal**
3 **tablespoons shortening**
¼ **cup molasses**
2 **teaspoons salt**
1 **package active dry yeast**
¼ **cup warm water (105 to 115°)**
1 **egg**
2¾ **cups all-purpose flour***

Grease loaf pan, 8½x4½x2¾ or 9x5x3 inches. In large mixer bowl, mix boiling water, the cornmeal, shortening, molasses and salt; cool to lukewarm.

Dissolve yeast in warm water. Add yeast, egg and half the flour to cornmeal mixture. Beat on medium speed 2 minutes, scraping bowl frequently, or beat 300 vigorous strokes by hand. Stir in remaining flour until smooth. Spread evenly in pan. Batter will be sticky; smooth top of loaf with floured hand.

Let rise in warm place until batter reaches top of 8½-inch pan or 1 inch from top of 9-inch pan, about 1½ hours. Sprinkle small amount of cornmeal and salt on loaf.

Heat oven to 375°. Bake until loaf sounds hollow when tapped, 50 to 55 minutes. Remove loaf from pan; place on wire rack. Brush top with melted butter or shortening. Cool before cutting. *1 loaf.*

*If using self-rising flour, omit salt.

Variations

Little Loaves: Grease 6 miniature loaf pans, 4½x 2½x1½ inches. Divide batter among pans and let rise until it just reaches the tops of pans, about 1½ hours. Bake 30 to 35 minutes.

Oatmeal Batter Bread: Substitute ½ cup oats for the yellow cornmeal.

CREAMY PEACH PUDDING

½ can (18-ounce size) vanilla pudding (1 cup)
¼ cup dairy sour cream
 1 can (8 ounces) sliced peaches, drained

Mix pudding and sour cream. Layer pudding and peaches in each dessert dish. *2 servings*.

QUICK MOCHA DESSERT

Mix ½ can (18-ounce size) chocolate pudding (1 cup) and 1½ teaspoons powdered instant coffee. Divide between dessert dishes and garnish with whipped topping and mint leaves. *2 servings*.

GINGER COOKIES

Heat oven to 375°. Mix 1 package (14.5 ounces) gingerbread mix and ½ cup water. Drop dough by teaspoonfuls about 2 inches apart onto lightly greased baking sheet. Bake until almost no imprint remains when touched, 10 to 12 minutes. *About 3 dozen cookies*.

Variation

Mincemeat Ginger Drops: Stir in 1 cup prepared mincemeat and ½ cup chopped nuts.

"Corned Beef Revisited": a clever variety show featuring robust Reuben sandwiches, a savory skillet hash, a reprise of corned beef and cabbage (only easier), a cheesy casserole (easier still).

CORNED BEEF SKILLET HASH

- 1 cup chopped cooked corned beef
- 1 cup chopped cooked potatoes
- ¼ cup finely chopped onion
- 1 tablespoon snipped parsley
- ¼ teaspoon salt
- ⅛ teaspoon pepper
- 3 tablespoons salad oil
- ½ cup tomato juice

Mix meat, potatoes, onion, parsley, salt and pepper. Heat oil in 8-inch skillet. Spread meat mixture evenly in skillet; brown over medium heat, turning frequently with wide spatula, about 10 minutes. Stir in tomato juice. Reduce heat; cover and cook until liquid is absorbed, about 10 minutes. *2 servings*.

REUBEN GRILL

- 2 tablespoons Thousand Island dressing
- 4 slices rye or pumpernickel bread
- 2 slices Swiss cheese
- ½ cup sauerkraut, drained
- ½ pound thinly sliced cooked corned beef
  Soft butter or margarine

Spread dressing on 2 slices bread. Top with cheese, sauerkraut, meat and remaining bread slices. Spread butter on outsides of sandwiches. Grill in skillet over low to medium heat until brown and cheese is melted, 5 to 7 minutes on each side. *2 servings*.

QUICK CORNED BEEF AND CABBAGE

  2 tablespoons butter or margarine
1½ cups coarsely shredded cabbage
  ½ package (5.5-ounce size) hash brown potatoes with
     onions (about 1¼ cups)
  ¾ cup water
  ½ teaspoon salt
  1 cup cut-up cooked corned beef

Melt butter in 8-inch skillet. Stir in cabbage, potatoes, water and salt. Cook over medium-high heat until liquid is absorbed and bottom is brown, 8 to 12 minutes. Sprinkle meat into skillet; turn mixture with wide spatula and cook until meat is hot, about 3 minutes. *2 servings.*

CORNED BEEF AND MACARONI CASSEROLE

Heat oven to 375°. Measure contents of 1 package (8 ounces) macaroni and Cheddar dinner; divide in half (approximately ¾ cup macaroni and ⅓ cup Cheese Sauce Mix).*

In ungreased, 1-quart casserole, mix half the macaroni, ⅓ cup Cheese Sauce Mix, 1½ teaspoons butter or margarine and 1¼ cups boiling water. Stir in 1 cup cut-up cooked corned beef. Cover and bake 20 to 25 minutes. Stir before serving. *2 servings.*

* To store remaining mix, close package securely and use within 2 weeks. Delicious with hamburgers, frankfurters, chicken or luncheon meat.

Variations

Tuna and Macaroni Casserole: Omit corned beef and stir in 1 can (6½ ounces) tuna, drained and flaked.

Chicken and Macaroni Casserole: Omit corned beef and stir in 1 can (5 ounces) boned chicken, cut up, and 2 tablespoons sliced pimiento-stuffed olives.

SOMETHING SPECIAL...

Carving Cues

Carving can be as easy as 1, 2, 3: 1—a good, sharp carving knife; 2—properly cooked meat; 3—a little practice.

Take good care of your knife—it's your most important tool. Store it sheathed or boxed to protect the edge, wash it (separately) after every use and always carve on a cutting board.

Be sure to let a roast "set" before carving (see spe-

Rolled Roast Secure roast with fork. Slice downward across grain of meat with straight, even strokes, making each slice about ¼ inch thick.

Flank Steak Always cut across grain of meat at a slanted angle into thin, even slices, keeping slices uniform in thickness.

Porterhouse Steak Cut around bone; remove. Carve 1-inch slices across width of steak. (Each serving should have a portion of the tenderloin.)

cific recipes). This allows the meat to become a little firmer and therefore easier to cut.

Just before the "setting" time is up, remember to remove all strings and skewers from the roast—though it's a good idea to leave one or two strings on a rolled roast so that it won't fall apart when you carve it.

Check which way the grain of the meat runs, then slice at right angles to the grain. This way the muscle fibers of each slice will be short—and the shorter the fibers, the more tender the meat. Flank steak, beef corned brisket and other cuts that are too thin to cut at right angles should be sliced at a slant across the grain. Whatever kind of meat you choose, try to carve slices that are uniform in size and thickness.

Pork Loin Roast Have re-tailer saw backbone free from ribs for easy carving; after cooking, remove bone. Cut slices on each side of rib bones.

Leg of Lamb Cut 2 or 3 slices from thin side; turn onto cut side. Make vertical slices to bone; cut horizontally along bone to free slices.

Turkey Remove leg. Make deep horizontal cut into breast above wing. Starting halfway up, carve thin slices to the cut, working upward.

Baked Ham
Pecan Sweet Potatoes
Cauliflower with Nutmeg Butter
Molded Lime-Pineapple Salad
Brown and Serve Rolls
Mocha Parfaits (page 87)

BAKED HAM

Place ham fat side up on rack in shallow roasting pan. Insert meat thermometer so tip is in center of thickest part of meat and does not touch bone or rest in fat.

Roast uncovered in 325° oven until done (see Time-table), using thermometer reading as final guide. Ham is easier to carve if allowed to "set" 15 to 20 minutes after removing from oven. Since meat continues to cook after removal from oven, if ham is to set, it should be removed when thermometer registers 5° lower than desired doneness.

PECAN SWEET POTATOES

Heat oven to 325°. Place 1 can (8 ounces) sweet potatoes in syrup, drained, in ungreased 1¾-cup casserole. Sprinkle with 3 tablespoons brown sugar and dot with 1 tablespoon butter. Bake uncovered until hot and bubbly, 25 to 30 minutes. Sprinkle with 1 to 2 tablespoons broken pecans. *2 servings.*

CAULIFLOWER WITH NUTMEG BUTTER

Heat 1 inch salted water (½ teaspoon salt to 1 cup water) to boiling. Add 1 small cauliflower. Cover; heat to boiling. Cook until tender, 12 to 15 minutes. Drain; turn into serving dish. Dot with butter and sprinkle with nutmeg. *2 servings.*

MOLDED LIME-PINEAPPLE SALAD

1 cup boiling water
1 package (3 ounces) lime-flavored gelatin
1 can (8¾ ounces) crushed pineapple, drained
   (reserve syrup)
   Lettuce
   Mayonnaise

Pour boiling water on gelatin in bowl; stir until gelatin is dissolved. Add enough water to reserved pineapple syrup to measure 1 cup; stir into gelatin. Chill until thickened but not set.

Stir in pineapple. Pour into 4 to 6 individual molds or one 4-cup mold. Chill until firm. Place 2 servings on lettuce and top each with mayonnaise. Serve remaining gelatin topped with whipped cream as a dessert the next day. *2 servings—and 2 to 4 for another day.*

TIMETABLE

Cut	Approximate Cooking Time (Minutes per Lb.)	Meat Thermometer Reading
Ham (fully cooked)		
Half		
5 to 7 lbs.	18 to 24	140°
Shank or rump (butt) portion		
3 to 4 lbs.	18 to 24	140°
Ham (cook before eating)		
Half		
5 to 7 lbs.	22 to 25	160°
Shank or rump (butt) portion		
· 3 to 4 lbs.	35 to 40	160°
Smoked Shoulder Roll		
2 to 4 lbs.	35 to 40	170°

Four impressive planned-overs from That Ham. Note
especially the unique Ham 'n Cheese Supper Bread.
Be sure to serve it warm, with soup and a jumbo
salad.

EGGS BENEDICT

2 eggs
1 envelope (1¼ ounces) hollandaise sauce mix
2 thin slices cooked ham
1 English muffin, split and toasted

Heat water (1½ to 2 inches) in saucepan or skillet to
boiling; reduce heat to simmer. Break eggs, 1 at a time,
into custard cup or saucer; holding cup or saucer close
to surface of water, slip egg into water. Cook until eggs
reach desired doneness, 3 to 5 minutes.

While eggs cook, prepare hollandaise sauce as directed on package. Place slice of ham on each muffin
half, then top with an egg and half the hollandaise
sauce. *2 servings.*

CHILI-BEAN SKILLET

1 cup cubed cooked ham
½ cup sliced celery
¼ cup chopped onion
¼ cup chopped green pepper
Dash instant minced garlic
½ teaspoon salt
2 tablespoons salad oil
1 can (8 ounces) pork and beans
1 can (8 ounces) lima beans
⅓ cup chili sauce

In 8-inch skillet, cook and stir ham, celery, onion,
green pepper, garlic and salt in oil until onion is tender.

Drain off fat. Stir in pork and beans, lima beans (with liquid) and chili sauce; simmer uncovered until hot, about 10 minutes. *2 servings.*

HAM 'N CHEESE SUPPER BREAD

- 1 cup buttermilk baking mix
- ½ cup chopped cooked ham
- 2 tablespoons instant minced onion
- 1 egg
- ⅓ cup milk
- 1 tablespoon salad oil
- ¼ teaspoon prepared mustard
- 1 cup shredded Cheddar cheese (about 4 ounces)
- 1 tablespoon sesame seed

Heat oven to 350°. Grease 1-quart casserole. Mix baking mix, ham, onion, egg, milk, oil, mustard and ⅔ cup of the cheese. Spread in casserole. Sprinkle remaining cheese and the sesame seed on top. Bake until top is golden brown, 30 to 35 minutes. Serve warm. *2 servings.*

Note: Wrap leftover bread in aluminum foil and refrigerate or freeze. Heat in wrapping in 400° oven until warm, about 10 minutes (if frozen, 30 to 35 minutes).

SCALLOPED POTATOES WITH HAM

Heat oven to 400°. Measure contents of 1 package (5.5 ounces) scalloped potatoes; divide in half (approximately 1 cup potato slices and 3 tablespoons sauce mix).* Place potato slices in ungreased 1-quart casserole; sprinkle half the sauce mix on potato slices. Add 1 cup cut-up cooked ham and stir in half the amounts of water and milk called for on package. Bake uncovered until potatoes are tender and golden brown, 25 to 30 minutes. *2 servings.*

* To store remaining mix, close package securely and use within 2 weeks. Make Hot Potato Salad (page 15) or prepare Quick Scalloped Potatoes (page 116) and serve with pork chops, ham, frankfurters or hamburgers.

**Roast Beef with Oven-browned Potatoes
Sautéed Cherry Tomatoes
Marinated Asparagus Spears
Lemon Sherbet with
Raspberry-Currant Sauce (page 67)**

ROAST BEEF WITH OVEN-BROWNED POTATOES

Place roast fat side up on rack in shallow roasting pan. Season with salt and pepper before, during or after roasting (salt goes into roast only ¼ to ½ inch). Insert meat thermometer so tip is in center of thickest part of meat and does not rest in fat.

Roast uncovered in 325° oven until done (see Timetable), using thermometer reading as final guide. About 1½ hours before roast is done, pare 2 medium baking potatoes. If you wish, make thin crosswise cuts almost through potatoes. Heat 1 inch salted water (½ teaspoon salt to 1 cup water) to boiling. Add potatoes. Cover and heat to boiling; cook 10 minutes. Drain.

Place potatoes in meat drippings in roasting pan; turn each potato to coat with fat. Or brush potatoes with melted butter or margarine and place on rack with meat. Turning potatoes once, bake until tender and golden brown, 1¼ to 1½ hours. Season with salt and pepper.

Roasts are easier to carve if allowed to "set" 15 to 20 minutes after removing from oven. Since meat continues to cook after removal from oven, if roast is to set, it should be removed from oven when thermometer registers 5° lower than the desired doneness. Serve with meat juices or Pan Gravy (page 92). *2 servings.*

TIMETABLE

Cut	Approximate Cooking Time (Minutes per Lb.)	Meat Thermometer Reading
Boneless Rib	32	140° (rare)
5 to 7 lbs.	38	160° (medium)
	48	170° (well)
Rib Eye	18 to 20	140° (rare)
(Delmonico)*	20 to 22	160° (medium)
4 to 5 lbs.	22 to 24	170° (well)
Tip Roast	35 to 40	150 to 170°
(high quality)		
3½ to 4 lbs.		
Rolled Rump	25 to 30	150 to 170°
(high quality)		
4 to 5 lbs.		

* Roast at 350°.

SAUTÉED CHERRY TOMATOES

Remove stem ends from ½ pint cherry tomatoes. Prick each tomato several times. Melt 1 tablespoon butter or margarine in 8-inch skillet. Cook and stir tomatoes in butter over medium heat until heated through, about 3 minutes. For a garnish, sprinkle snipped chives on top. *2 servings.*

MARINATED ASPARAGUS SPEARS

 1 package (10 ounces) frozen asparagus spears
½ cup Italian dressing
   Lettuce leaves
   Pimiento strips

Cook asparagus spears as directed on package. Drain and turn into bowl. Pour dressing on hot asparagus; cover and refrigerate 2 to 3 hours. Serve spears on lettuce leaves and garnish with pimiento strips. *2 servings.*

Now revel in your beef leftovers! Savor Beef Rolls in Wine, a recipe you may well want to double to share with a pair of discriminating friends. Enjoy a superb main-dish salad. And by all means, get familiar with the quick skillet dish—it lets you shine even when you've plain run out of time!

CHILI CHEF'S SALAD

½ cup julienne strips cooked meat (beef, ham, tongue, luncheon meat)
½ cup julienne strips cooked chicken or turkey
½ cup julienne strips Swiss cheese
¼ cup chopped green onion
¼ cup sliced celery
8 cups bite-size pieces lettuce (iceberg and/or romaine)
⅓ cup mayonnaise or salad dressing
⅓ cup chili sauce
Ripe olives
1 hard-cooked egg, cut into wedges

Reserve few strips of meat, chicken and cheese for garnish. In large bowl, toss remaining meat, chicken, cheese, the onion, celery and lettuce. Mix mayonnaise and chili sauce; pour on salad and toss. Garnish with reserved meat, chicken and cheese, the olives and egg wedges. *2 generous servings.*

HERBED BEEF AND ONIONS

2 tablespoons butter or margarine
1 medium onion, sliced and separated into rings
4 slices cooked roast beef
2 teaspoons vinegar
1 tablespoon butter or margarine, softened
⅛ teaspoon thyme, tarragon or marjoram leaves

Melt 2 tablespoons butter in 8-inch skillet; cook and stir onion until tender, about 5 minutes. Remove onion from skillet and keep warm.

Add meat to skillet; brown quickly on both sides and sprinkle with vinegar. Mix 1 tablespoon butter and the thyme leaves. Arrange meat and onions on dinner plates; top meat with seasoned butter. *2 servings.*

BEEF ROLLS IN WINE

- 1 can (2 ounces) mushroom stems and pieces, drained and chopped
- 2 tablespoons chopped onion
- 4 thin slices cooked roast beef
- 1 tablespoon salad oil
- 1 can (16 ounces) whole carrots, drained (reserve liquid)
- 3 tablespoons red wine
- 3 tablespoons gravy mix (dry)
- ¼ teaspoon salt
- ¼ teaspoon pepper
  Dash thyme
  Snipped parsley

Mix mushrooms and onion; place ¼ of mixture on center of each beef slice. Roll up and fasten with wooden picks. Heat oil in 8-inch skillet; brown rolls. Add enough water to reserved carrot liquid to measure 1 cup. Stir carrot liquid, wine, gravy mix, salt, pepper and thyme into skillet. Heat to boiling. Reduce heat; cover and simmer 10 minutes. Add carrots; simmer until hot, about 10 minutes. Garnish with parsley. *2 servings.*

> **Roast Pork**
> **Herbed Brussels Sprouts**
> **Country-style Waldorf Salad**
> **Yeast Rolls (page 50)**
> **Lemon Pudding Cake**

ROAST PORK

Place roast fat side up on rack in shallow roasting pan. Season with salt and pepper before, during or after roasting (salt goes into roast only ¼ to ½ inch). Insert meat thermometer so tip is in center of thickest part of meat and does not touch bone or rest in fat.

Roast uncovered in 325° oven until done (see Timetable), using thermometer reading as final guide. Roasts are easier to carve if allowed to "set" 15 to 20 minutes after removing from oven. Since meat continues to cook after removal from oven, if roast is to set, it should be removed from oven when thermometer registers 5° lower than the desired doneness.

TIMETABLE

Cut	Approximate Cooking Time (Minutes per Lb.)	Meat Thermometer Reading
Loin		
Center		
3 to 5 lbs.	30 to 35	170°
Blade		
5 to 7 lbs.	35 to 40	170°
Sirloin		
3 to 4 lbs.	40 to 45	170°
Boneless Top (double)		
3 to 5 lbs.	35 to 45	170°
Boneless Top		
2 to 4 lbs.	30 to 35	170°

HERBED BRUSSELS SPROUTS

Cook 1 package (10 ounces) frozen Brussels sprouts as directed. Drain. Add 1 tablespoon butter or margarine and ⅛ teaspoon dill weed, caraway seed or marjoram leaves and toss. *2 servings.*

COUNTRY-STYLE WALDORF SALAD

½ **cup diced unpared apple (about ½ apple)**
⅓ **cup diced celery**
¼ **cup halved seedless green grapes**
2 **tablespoons coarsely chopped nuts**
1 **cup bite-size pieces lettuce**
¼ **cup mayonnaise or salad dressing**

Toss all ingredients in bowl. Garnish salad with unpared apple slices. *2 servings.*

LEMON PUDDING CAKE

1 **egg, separated**
1 **teaspoon grated lemon peel**
2 **tablespoons lemon juice**
⅓ **cup milk**
½ **cup sugar**
2 **tablespoons flour**
⅛ **teaspoon salt**

Heat oven to 325°. Beat egg white until stiff peaks form. Beat egg yolk; add remaining ingredients and beat until smooth. Fold in egg white.

Divide between ungreased 1-cup baking dishes or 6-ounce custard cups. Place in pan of hot water (1 inch deep). Bake 45 to 50 minutes. Serve warm, with whipped cream if you like. *2 generous servings.*

Applause from the audience as pork stages a come-back. Star it in an Oriental show of chow mein or a speedy meal-in-a-skillet. And for a final bow, a casserole that calls for your can opener and oven to do most of the work.

PORK CHOW MEIN

1 tablespoon salad oil or shortening
1 to 1½ cups cubed cooked pork
1 small onion, chopped (about ¼ cup)
1 cup water
1 teaspoon instant chicken bouillon
¼ teaspoon garlic salt
1 can (about 3 ounces) sliced mushrooms, drained (reserve liquid)
1 tablespoon soy sauce
2 tablespoons cornstarch
1 can (16 ounces) Chinese vegetables, drained
Chow mein noodles

Heat oil in 8-inch skillet; brown meat and push to one side. Add onion; cook and stir until onion is tender. Stir in water, bouillon and garlic salt; heat to boiling. Reduce heat; cover and simmer 5 minutes.

Blend reserved mushroom liquid, soy sauce and cornstarch; stir into meat mixture. Add mushrooms and Chinese vegetables. Cook, stirring constantly, until mixture thickens and boils. Boil and stir 1 minute. Serve on noodles, and if you like, with additional soy sauce. *2 servings.*

Variations

Beef, Chicken or Turkey Chow Mein: Substitute 1 to 1½ cups cubed cooked beef, chicken or turkey for the pork.

CHINESE PORK AND RICE

⅓ cup uncooked regular rice
¼ cup chopped onion
1 stalk celery, cut into diagonal slices
1 tablespoon salad oil
¾ cup water
1 teaspoon instant chicken or beef bouillon
1 tablespoon soy sauce
1 cup cut-up cooked pork (¾-inch pieces)
½ green pepper, chopped

In 8-inch skillet, cook and stir rice, onion and celery in oil over medium heat until rice is golden brown and onion is tender. Stir in water, bouillon, soy sauce and meat; heat to boiling, stirring occasionally. Reduce heat; cover tightly and simmer until rice is tender, 12 to 15 minutes. Stir in green pepper; cover and simmer until liquid is absorbed and pepper is crisp-tender, about 5 minutes. *2 servings.*

SAUCY PORK 'N NOODLE BAKE

1 tablespoon salad oil
1 cup cut-up cooked pork
½ cup uncooked noodles
1 can (10½ ounces) condensed cream of chicken soup
1 can (8 ounces) whole kernel corn, drained
1 tablespoon sliced pimiento
½ cup shredded sharp Cheddar cheese
¼ cup finely diced green pepper

Heat oven to 375°. Heat oil in 8-inch skillet; brown meat over medium-high heat. Drain off fat. Stir in remaining ingredients. Pour into ungreased 1-quart casserole. Bake uncovered until noodles are tender, about 45 minutes. *2 generous servings.*

Celery Victor
Roast Turkey
Giblet Gravy
Cranberry Sauce
Mashed Potatoes
Broccoli with Lemon Butter
Hot Cloverleaf Rolls
Pumpkin Custards

CELERY VICTOR

1 bunch celery
1 cup water
1 teaspoon instant beef bouillon
⅓ cup Italian dressing

Trim off root end of celery bunch but do not separate stalks. Remove leaves and coarse outer stalks; reserve some leaves for garnish. Cut celery bunch crosswise so bottom section is 3 inches long. (Refrigerate top section for future use.) Cut bottom section crosswise in half; tie halves with string.

In small saucepan, heat water and bouillon to boiling. Add celery halves; heat to boiling. Cover and cook until tender, about 15 minutes. Drain. Place celery halves in shallow 1-quart casserole; pour dressing on halves. Refrigerate 3 hours, spooning dressing on halves 2 or 3 times. Place celery half on each salad plate; remove string. Garnish with pimiento strips and celery leaves. *2 servings.*

ROAST TURKEY

Choose a 4- to 8-pound fryer-roaster turkey. If turkey is frozen, thaw as directed on package. Wash turkey and pat dry.

If turkey is to be stuffed, stuff just before roasting. Use ½ package (7-ounce size) herbed stuffing and half the amounts of butter and water called for on package; prepare as directed. Fill wishbone area with stuffing first; fasten neck skin to back with skewer.

Fold wings across back with tips touching. Fill body cavity lightly. (Do not pack—stuffing will expand while cooking.) Tuck drumsticks under band of skin at tail or tie together with heavy string, then tie to tail.

Place turkey breast side up on rack in shallow roasting pan. Brush with butter, salad oil or shortening. Insert meat thermometer so tip is in thickest part of inside thigh muscle or thickest part of breast meat and does not touch bone.

Roast uncovered in 325° oven, brushing occasionally with butter or pan drippings, until tender, 2½ to 3½ hours. If turkey is browning too quickly, cover loosely with aluminum foil. Meat thermometer should register 180 to 185°. Or test for doneness by pressing thickest part of the drumstick between protected fingers —if done, the meat should feel very soft. Or move drumstick up and down—if done, the joint should give readily or break.

When turkey is done, remove from oven and allow to stand about 20 minutes for easiest carving. Serve with Giblet Gravy (page 166) if you wish.

Remove every bit of stuffing from turkey as soon as possible after serving. Cool stuffing, meat and any gravy promptly; refrigerate separately. Use gravy or stuffing within 1 or 2 days; heat them thoroughly before serving. Serve cooked turkey meat within 2 or 3 days after roasting. If frozen, it can be kept up to 1 month.

GIBLET GRAVY

While turkey is roasting, cook giblets: In small saucepan, heat gizzard, heart, neck, ¼ teaspoon salt, 2 peppercorns, 1 bay leaf and enough water to cover to boiling. Reduce heat; cover and simmer until gizzard is fork tender, about 1 hour. Add liver during last 15 minutes of cooking. Remove meat from neck; finely chop giblets and reserve broth.

Pour drippings from roasting pan into bowl, leaving brown particles in pan. Return 1 tablespoon drippings to pan. Mix in 1 tablespoon flour. Cook over low heat, stirring until mixture is smooth and bubbly. Remove from heat. Stir in ½ cup of the reserved broth. Heat to boiling, stirring constantly. Boil and stir 1 minute. Stir in giblets and heat through. *About ¾ cup.*

MASHED POTATOES

  3 **medium potatoes (about 1 pound)**
    About ¼ cup milk
  2 **tablespoons soft butter or margarine**
¼ **teaspoon salt**
    Dash pepper

Pare potatoes. Heat 1 inch salted water (½ teaspoon salt to 1 cup water) to boiling. Add potatoes. Cover and heat to boiling; cook until tender—30 to 35 minutes for whole potatoes, 20 to 25 minutes for cut. Drain. Gently shake pan over low heat to dry potatoes.

   Mash potatoes until no lumps remain. Add milk in small amounts, beating after each addition. (Amount of milk needed to make potatoes smooth and fluffy depends on kind of potatoes.) Add butter, salt and pepper; beat until potatoes are light and fluffy. Dot with butter or sprinkle paprika or snipped parsley on top. *2 servings.*

PUMPKIN CUSTARDS

½ **can (16-ounce size) pumpkin pie mix***
  1 **egg, slightly beaten**
½ **cup milk**
    Streusel Topping (below)

Heat oven to 325°. Mix pie mix, egg and milk until smooth. Pour into 2 ungreased 10-ounce custard cups. Sprinkle Streusel Topping on top. Place cups in baking pan, 9x9x2 inches; pour very hot water into pan to within ½ inch of tops of cups.

   Bake until knife inserted halfway between center and edge comes out clean, about 1 hour. Remove cups from water. Serve warm or chilled. *2 servings.*

Streusel Topping

¼ cup brown sugar (packed)
2 tablespoons flour
2 tablespoons chopped pecans
¼ teaspoon cinnamon
2 tablespoons soft butter or margarine

Mix all ingredients with fork until crumbly.

* Leftover pumpkin pie mix? Use in Frosty Pumpkin Custard (page 61).

Look what you can do for a turkey encore: salads, sandwiches, a quick one-dish dinner. Take off from there. Have fun!

HOT TURKEY SUPPER SALAD

1 cup cut-up cooked turkey
1 cup thinly sliced celery
½ cup croutons
½ cup mayonnaise
¼ cup diced roasted almonds
1 tablespoon lemon juice
1 teaspoon onion salt
¼ cup shredded Cheddar cheese
½ cup croutons or crushed potato chips

Heat oven to 350°. Mix all ingredients except cheese and ½ cup croutons. Divide between 2 ungreased 1½-cup casseroles. Sprinkle cheese and ½ cup croutons on tops. Bake 20 to 25 minutes. *2 servings.*

BROILED TURKEY AND CHEESE SANDWICHES

1 package (10 ounces) frozen asparagus spears or broccoli spears
2 tablespoons deviled ham, if desired
2 slices toast, buttered
  Sliced cooked turkey
2 slices process American cheese

Cook asparagus spears as directed on package. Drain. Spread 1 tablespoon ham on each slice toast. Top with turkey slices, half the asparagus spears and a cheese slice.

Set oven control at broil and/or 550°. Broil sandwiches with tops 6 inches from heat just until cheese is bubbly, about 1 minute. Watch carefully! *2 servings.*

TURKEY CREOLE

> 1 small onion, thinly sliced
> ½ small green pepper, cut into narrow strips
> ¼ cup thinly sliced celery
> 1 tablespoon salad oil
> 1 can (8 ounces) stewed tomatoes
> 1 can (8 ounces) tomato sauce
> 1 to 1½ teaspoons chili powder
> ¼ teaspoon salt
> 1½ cups cut-up cooked turkey
>   Hot cooked rice or spaghetti

In 8-inch skillet, cook and stir onion, green pepper and celery in oil until vegetables are tender, about 5 minutes. Stir in tomatoes, tomato sauce, chili powder and salt; simmer uncovered 10 minutes. Stir in turkey; cover and simmer until turkey is hot, about 5 minutes. Serve on rice. *2 servings*.

BACON-TURKEY CLUB SALAD

> 6 cups bite-size pieces lettuce
> 4 to 5 slices bacon, crisply fried and crumbled
> 1 medium tomato, cut into wedges
> 1½ cups cut-up cooked turkey
> 1 hard-cooked egg, sliced
>   Barbecue Dressing (below)

Toss lettuce, bacon, tomato and turkey in bowl. Garnish with egg slices. Serve with dressing. *2 servings*.

Barbecue Dressing

> ¼ cup mayonnaise or salad dressing
> 2 tablespoons barbecue sauce
> 2 teaspoons instant minced onion
> 2 teaspoons lemon juice
> ¼ teaspoon salt
> ⅛ teaspoon pepper

Mix all ingredients. *About ⅓ cup*.

SOMETHING SPECIAL...

Freezing Tips

Freezing ABC's

Hurry! Moving fast is the first secret of successful freezing. Cool cooked foods quickly (small amounts in the refrigerator, larger portions in a bowl of ice and water). Then wrap and rush to the freezer. Hurry home with the frozens you buy. For anything frozen or to-be-frozen, the zero hour is now!

Pack properly. It's critical. Any already-frozen food can be transferred to your own freezer without re-wrapping. But if you're starting from scratch, be sure to use the wraps that are specially designed for freezing. Wrap tightly, pressing out all air; seal with tape. Or easier, use heavy-duty freezer bags. Again, press out air bubbles and seal securely with twist closures. If you use freezer containers, (for stews, casseroles and the like), allow plenty of headspace. Food expands in freezing.

Identify. Use a felt pen or grease pencil to note the following on freezer tape:

• What's in the package
• Date by which it should be used

Freeze at zero . . . or below. The lower the temperature, the faster foods freeze. And the faster they freeze, the less apt they are to lose flavor and texture. An even, low temperature is also a must for *keeping* foods in prime condition.

Freezing for Two

Extras. No matter how smartly you shop, cooking for two always seems to produce an excess bit of this or that. For short-term storage, use little see-through plastic bags to freeze dabs of chopped onion, chopped green pepper, drained pimiento, nuts, grated cheese, grated peels—and put those leftovers to work.

Excesses. Plan around them. Cook a big piece of meat. Cool the leftovers quickly. Cover and refrigerate right away (to use within 1 or 2 days). Or freeze in meal-size portions: Most cooked meats and poultry can be frozen up to 1 month—up to 6 months if frozen with broth or gravy. Allow to thaw (still freezer-wrapped) in the refrigerator. See recipes in this chapter for ways to use leftover meat. For specifics on uncooked meat, poultry and fish, see pages 223–231.

Stews, Chili and Sauces

Before freezing: Do not overcook. Keep spice level low. Avoid potatoes—they don't freeze well. Cool quickly. Leave headspace in container to allow for expansion.

Maximum storage: 3 to 4 months.

To reheat: Heat slowly in saucepan 20 to 30 minutes, stirring occasionally; add liquid if necessary.

Breads

Before freezing: Wrap rolls and French bread in meal-size portions. (French bread can be sliced and buttered first.) Bakery bread can be frozen in its store wrap—overwrap if it is to be stored longer than 3 months. (A slice of bread will thaw in 10 minutes.)

Maximum storage: 2 to 3 months for biscuits, muffins, nut breads (quick breads); 9 months for yeast breads and rolls.

To reheat: Leave in foil wrap and heat in 350° oven (20 to 25 minutes if frozen, 10 minutes if thawed). Frozen sliced bread can be toasted.

Cakes and Cupcakes

Before freezing: Wrap whole or in serving pieces. (Frozen cake can be sliced easily.) Freeze frosted cakes uncovered, then wrap.

Maximum storage: 2 to 3 months if frosted; 4 to 6 months if unfrosted.

To thaw: Leave in freezer wrap. Let unfrosted cakes stand at room temperature 2 to 3 hours (about 30 minutes for cupcakes); place frosted cakes, loosely covered, in refrigerator.

Cookies

Before freezing: Place cool cookies in airtight container or freezer wrap.

Maximum storage: 9 to 12 months.

To thaw: Let cookies stand at room temperature.

TWO IS COMPANY

**Memory-making dinners that say,
"Tonight is special"**

Crab-Ham Roll-ups with Curry Sauce
Parsleyed Rice (page 182)
Peas and Celery
Marinated Artichoke Salad
Brandied Cherry Sundaes

CRAB-HAM ROLL-UPS WITH CURRY SAUCE

1 package (6 ounces) frozen cooked crabmeat
6 thin slices boiled ham (about ¼ pound)
1 envelope (about 1½ ounces) white sauce mix
¼ teaspoon curry powder
1 teaspoon sherry or sherry flavoring
Parsleyed Rice (page 182)
Sliced green onion or capers

Heat oven to 350°. Cut frozen crabmeat into 6 sticks.
Place frozen stick at narrow end of each ham slice;
roll up and secure with wooden pick. Place seam side
down in ungreased baking pan, 9x9x2 inches. Cover
and bake until hot, about 20 minutes.

While ham rolls bake, prepare white sauce as directed on package except—stir in curry powder and
sherry. Arrange ham rolls on rice; spoon half the sauce
onto rolls and sprinkle with onion. Serve with remaining sauce. *2 servings.*

Note: 1 can (7½ ounces) crabmeat, drained and
cartilage removed, can be substituted for the frozen
cooked crabmeat.

PEAS AND CELERY

½ package (10-ounce size) frozen green peas
¼ cup sliced celery
1 tablespoon soft butter or margarine

Cook peas and celery as directed on package for peas except—use only half the amounts of water and salt called for. Drain. Dot with butter and toss. *2 servings.*

MARINATED ARTICHOKE SALAD

1 jar (6 ounces) marinated artichoke hearts, drained
¼ cup ripe olive halves
1 small onion, sliced and separated into rings
  Salad greens
  Oil-and-vinegar dressing

Arrange artichoke hearts, olives and onion rings on salad greens. Serve with oil-and-vinegar dressing. *2 servings.*

BRANDIED CHERRY SUNDAES

Heat 1 can (8 ounces) pitted dark sweet cherries. Stir in 1 teaspoon brandy flavoring or brandy. Divide ½ can (18-ounce size) vanilla pudding or ½ pint vanilla ice cream between dessert dishes. Spoon warm cherry sauce on pudding. Serve immediately. *2 servings.*

Classic Beef Stroganoff
Poppy Seed Noodles
Cherry Tomato-Brussels Sprouts Salad
Hot Crusty Rolls
Peaches Flambé

CLASSIC BEEF STROGANOFF

½ to ¾ pound beef sirloin or round steak, about
   ½ inch thick
2 tablespoons butter or margarine
¼ pound mushrooms, sliced, or 1 can (4½ ounces)
   sliced mushrooms, drained
1 small onion, finely chopped (about ¼ cup)
½ cup water
1 beef bouillon cube
1 tablespoon catsup
1 small clove garlic, finely chopped, or ⅛ teaspoon
   instant minced garlic
½ teaspoon salt
  Poppy Seed Noodles (below)
¼ cup water
1 tablespoon flour
½ cup dairy sour cream

Cut meat into strips, 1½ x ½ inch. Melt butter in 8
inch skillet; cook and stir mushrooms and onion until
onion is tender. Remove vegetables from skillet.

In same skillet, brown meat over medium heat. Stir
in ½ cup water, the bouillon cube, catsup, garlic and
salt. Reduce heat; cover and simmer 15 minutes (45
minutes if using round steak; if necessary, add small
amount of water). While meat simmers, prepare Poppy
Seed Noodles.

Mix ¼ cup water and the flour; stir into meat mixture. Add mushrooms and onion. Heat to boiling, stirring constantly. Boil and stir 1 minute. Stir in sour
cream and heat through. Serve on the noodles. *2 servings.*

POPPY SEED NOODLES

Cook 4 ounces noodles (about 1½ cups) in 1 quart boiling salted water (2 teaspoons salt) until tender, about 7 minutes. Drain noodles and return to saucepan. Add 1 tablespoon butter or margarine and 1 teaspoon poppy seed and toss.

CHERRY TOMATO-BRUSSELS SPROUTS SALAD

½ package (10-ounce size) frozen Brussels sprouts*
¼ cup oil-and-vinegar dressing or Italian dressing
1 cup cherry tomatoes
2 lettuce cups

Cook Brussels sprouts as directed except—use only half the amounts of water and salt called for on package. Drain. Pour dressing on hot Brussels sprouts. Cover and refrigerate at least 3 hours.

Cut tomatoes into halves; add to Brussels sprouts and toss. Serve in lettuce cups. *2 servings.*

* Leftover frozen Brussels sprouts? Serve later in the week as the vegetable at another meal. Especially good with ham, pork or turkey.

PEACHES FLAMBÉ

Vanilla ice cream
2 tablespoons apricot jam
2 tablespoons sugar
¼ cup water
½ teaspoon lemon juice
1 can (8¾ ounces) sliced peaches, drained
2 tablespoons brandy

Scoop ice cream into balls; place in freezer while preparing sauce. In small chafing dish or saucepan, heat jam, sugar, water and lemon juice, stirring occasionally, until syrupy, about 5 minutes. Add peaches and heat through. Heat brandy until warm; pour on peaches and ignite immediately. Spoon peaches and sauce on ice cream. *2 servings.*

Scallops en Brochette
Orange Rice
Melon-Cucumber Salad
Poppy Seed Rolls
Coconut Brûlée

SCALLOPS EN BROCHETTE

½ pound fresh or frozen scallops
½ can (8-ounce size) water chestnuts (about 12)*
3 slices bacon, each cut into 4 pieces and partially fried
½ green pepper, cut into chunks
1 firm medium tomato, cut into wedges, or 8 cherry
   tomatoes
2 tablespoons soy sauce
1 teaspoon brown sugar
⅛ teaspoon garlic powder

Thaw scallops if frozen; if large sea scallops are used
cut each into 3 or 4 pieces. Wash and remove any shel
particles. Alternate scallops, water chestnuts, bacon
green pepper and tomatoes on each of 4 skewers. Mi:
soy sauce, brown sugar and garlic powder.

Set oven control at broil and/or 550°. Broil bro
chettes with tops about 3 inches from heat, turnin
once and basting with soy sauce mixture, until baco
is crisp and scallops are light brown, 5 to 8 minutes
2 servings.

* Leftover water chestnuts? Slice and add to gree
beans, peas, Chinese pea pods or green salads. Or us
in Chinese Lamb Suey (page 143).

ORANGE RICE

Cook instant rice as directed on package for 2 serving:
except—substitute orange juice for half the water. Gar
nish with orange slices and parsley. *2 servings.*

MELON-CUCUMBER SALAD

2 tablespoons salad oil
1 tablespoon lemon juice
½ teaspoon sugar
¼ teaspoon salt
Dash freshly ground pepper
1 small cucumber, thinly sliced
1 cup ¾-inch pieces melon (honeydew, cantaloupe, watermelon)
Crisp salad greens

Mix oil, lemon juice, sugar, salt and pepper. Toss cucumber slices, melon and oil mixture in bowl; chill. Remove with slotted spoon to salad greens. *2 servings.*

Variation

Pear-Cucumber Salad: Substitute 1 cup cut-up pears for the melon.

COCONUT BRÛLÉE

½ can (18-ounce size) vanilla pudding (1 cup)
2 teaspoons butter or margarine, melted
2 tablespoons brown sugar
2 tablespoons flaked coconut

Divide pudding between 2 individual baking dishes or 6-ounce custard cups. Mix butter, sugar and coconut; spoon onto pudding.

Set oven control at broil and/or 550°. Broil pudding with tops 5 inches from heat until coconut is golden and topping is bubbly, about 1½ minutes. Serve warm. *2 servings.*

Herb-roasted Chicken
Parsleyed Mixed Vegetables
Hot Crusty Rolls
Crêpes Suzette

HERB-ROASTED CHICKEN

2½- to 3-pound broiler-fryer chicken
¼ cup butter or margarine, melted
¼ teaspoon rosemary
¼ teaspoon thyme
¼ teaspoon marjoram
Parsleyed Mixed Vegetables (below)
Parsley

Heat oven to 375°. Rub cavity of chicken with salt i
desired. Place chicken breast side up on rack in roast
ing pan. Mix butter, rosemary, thyme and marjoram
brush half the herb-butter mixture on chicken. Roas
uncovered until done, 1¼ to 1¾ hours, brushing
chicken with remaining herb-butter mixture severa
times. If chicken is browning too quickly, cover loosely
with aluminum foil. Chicken is done when drumstick
meat feels very soft when pressed. Place chicken on
heated platter; surround with vegetables and garnish
with parsley. *2 servings.*

PARSLEYED MIXED VEGETABLES

   4 small or 2 medium potatoes, pared
   2 medium carrots, cut lengthwise into halves
   2 small onions
   ½ teaspoon seasoned salt
   ¼ cup water or chicken broth
   2 small zucchini, cut lengthwise into quarters
   ½ teaspoon seasoned salt
      Snipped parsley

Heat oven to 375°. If using medium potatoes, cut each in half. Combine all ingredients except zucchini, ½ teaspoon seasoned salt and the parsley in ungreased 1-quart casserole. Cover and bake 50 minutes. Add zucchini and salt; bake until vegetables are done, about 10 minutes. Arrange vegetables on platter; spoon on some liquid and sprinkle with parsley. *2 servings.*

CRÊPES SUZETTE

   Crêpes (below)
   ¼ cup butter or margarine
   ¼ teaspoon grated orange peel
   ¼ cup orange juice
   1 tablespoon sugar
   2 tablespoons orange-flavored liqueur or 2 tablespoons brandy

Prepare Crêpes. In 8-inch skillet, heat butter, orange peel, orange juice and sugar to boiling, stirring occasionally. Boil and stir 1 minute. Reduce heat. Fold crêpes into fourths; place in hot orange sauce, turning crêpes once.

   To flame, heat orange-flavored liqueur just until warm in long-handled ladle or small pan. Ignite and pour flaming over crêpes in skillet. Place 2 crêpes on each dessert plate; spoon sauce on crêpes. *2 servings.*

Crêpes

½ **cup all-purpose flour**
1 **teaspoon sugar**
¼ **teaspoon baking powder**
¼ **teaspoon salt**
⅔ **cup milk**
1 **egg**
¼ **teaspoon vanilla**
2 **teaspoons butter or margarine, melted**

Beat all ingredients with rotary beater until smooth. For each crêpe, lightly butter 8-inch skillet; heat over medium heat until butter is bubbly. Pour scant ¼ cup batter into skillet; immediately rotate pan until batter covers bottom. Cook until light brown; turn and brown other side. Stack crêpes so first-baked side is down. Cool, keeping crêpes covered to prevent them from drying out. *4 to 6 crêpes.*

As soon as you pour the crêpe batter into the skillet, quickly rotate the pan so that the batter covers the bottom evenly.

The tissue-thin crêpe can be lifted easily. Check the color of the bottom to see if it's time to turn it—it should be light brown.

Dim the lights, the bring out the crêpes in their orange sauce and flame them at the table for a triumphant finale to your dinner.

> **Cornish Hens Parisian**
> **Crisp Vegetable Dippers with Hollandaise Sauce**
> **French Bread**
> **Pears and Cheese**
> **Chocolate Mints**
> **Champagne**

CORNISH HENS PARISIAN

Thaw 2 frozen Rock Cornish hens (about 1 pound each). Heat oven to 350°. Rub cavities of hens with salt and pepper. Place breast side up on rack in shallow roasting pan. Brush Sauce Parisian (below) on hens. Roast uncovered until tender, about 1 hour, brushing sauce on hens 3 or 4 times. Chill thoroughly. *2 servings*.

Sauce Parisian

¼ cup butter or margarine
¼ cup vermouth or other dry white wine
½ teaspoon garlic salt
½ teaspoon onion salt

In small saucepan, heat all ingredients to boiling. *About ½ cup*.

Lamb Shish Kabobs
Parsleyed Rice
Greek Salad
Sesame Hard Rolls
Raspberry Crème
Almond Cookies

LAMB SHISH KABOBS

¾ **pound boneless lamb shoulder, cut into 1-inch cubes**
¼ **cup Caesar dressing or French dressing**
1 **can (8 ounces) whole onions, drained**
 About 8 pineapple chunks
 Green pepper pieces (½ pepper)
 Red pepper pieces (½ pepper)
 Parsleyed Rice (below)

Place meat in glass bowl; pour dressing on meat. Cover and refrigerate at least 8 hours.

Remove meat from marinade; reserve marinade. Alternate meat cubes, onions, pineapple chunks and green and red pepper pieces on each of 4 skewers. Set oven control at broil and/or 550°. Place skewers on rack in broiler pan. Brush some of the reserved marinade on kabobs. Broil with tops 4 to 5 inches from heat until meat is brown, about 6 minutes. Turn; brush remaining marinade on kabobs. Broil until done, about 5 minutes. Serve kabobs on Parsleyed Rice. *2 servings.*

PARSLEYED RICE

Cook instant rice as directed on package for 2 servings. Stir in 1 tablespoon snipped parsley.

GREEK SALAD

2 small heads Bibb lettuce
1 medium tomato, cut into wedges
6 pitted ripe olives
⅛ teaspoon oregano
1 tablespoon crumbled feta cheese or blue cheese
Lemon-Oil Dressing (below)
Lemon wedges

Place 1 head Bibb lettuce on each salad plate. Arrange tomato wedges and olives between leaves. Sprinkle oregano and cheese on salads; drizzle with dressing. Garnish salads with lemon wedges. *2 servings*.

Lemon-Oil Dressing

¼ cup olive oil or salad oil
1 tablespoon lemon juice
⅛ teaspoon salt
Dash pepper

Shake all ingredients in tightly covered jar. *About ¼ cup*.

RASPBERRY CRÈME

Mix 1 carton (8 ounces) raspberry yogurt and ½ cup frozen whipped topping (thawed). Divide between dessert dishes. Top with a dollop of whipped topping and garnish with mint leaves. *2 servings*.

> **Pheasant en Crème**
> **Wild Rice**
> **Sautéed Tomatoes**
> **Orange-Bermuda Onion Salad**
> **Breadsticks**
> **Blueberry Sundaes Jubilee**

PHEASANT EN CREME

- 1 pheasant, quartered
- 1 can (10½ ounces) condensed cream of chicken soup
- ½ cup apple cider
- 1 tablespoon plus 1 teaspoon Worcestershire sauce
- ¾ teaspoon salt
- ⅓ cup chopped onion
- 1 clove garlic, minced
- 1 can (3 ounces) sliced mushrooms, drained
  Paprika

Heat oven to 350°. Place pheasant in ungreased baking pan, 9x9x2 inches. Mix all ingredients except paprika; pour on pheasant.

Bake uncovered 1 hour, spooning off excess fat and basting once with sauce in pan. Sprinkle with paprika and bake until tender, about 30 minutes. *2 servings.*

Variation

Chicken en Crème: Substitute 2-pound broiler-fryer chicken for the pheasant.

WILD RICE

- 2 tablespoons butter or margarine
- ½ cup uncooked wild rice
- 2 tablespoons slivered almonds
- 2 tablespoons chopped onion
- 1½ cups boiling water
- 2 chicken bouillon cubes

Heat oven to 350°. Melt butter in 8-inch skillet. Cook and stir rice, almonds and onion in butter until almonds are golden, about 10 minutes. Stir in water and bouillon cubes. Pour into ungreased 2½-cup casserole. Cover with aluminum foil and bake until all liquid is absorbed and rice is tender and fluffy, about 1 hour 15 minutes. *2 servings.*

SAUTÉED TOMATOES

  2 **medium ripe or green tomatoes**
  3 **tablespoons butter or margarine**
  1 **egg, beaten**
½ **cup dry bread crumbs**
    Salt and pepper

Cut thin slices from ends of tomatoes; cut tomatoes into ¾-inch slices. Melt butter in large skillet. Dip slices into egg, then coat with bread crumbs. Cook in butter, turning once, until golden brown. Season with salt and pepper. *2 servings.*

ORANGE-BERMUDA ONION SALAD

Alternate slices of orange and rings of Bermuda onion. Top with Ruby-red Dressing (page 65).

BLUEBERRY SUNDAES JUBILEE

Prepare Blueberry Sauce (below). Soak 2 sugar cubes in orange extract. Spoon sauce on scoops of ice cream in dessert dishes. Top each with sugar cube and ignite. *2 servings.*

Blueberry Sauce

  1 **cup fresh or frozen blueberries**
  2 **tablespoons water**
  2 **tablespoons sugar**
  1 **tablespoon lemon juice**
  1 **teaspoon cornstarch**
¼ **teaspoon cinnamon**

Heat all ingredients to boiling, stirring constantly. Reduce heat; simmer 5 minutes, stirring occasionally. Serve warm or cool. *About ⅔ cup.*

> **Steak Diane**
> **Potato Soufflé**
> **Buttered Asparagus Spears**
> **Tomatoes Vinaigrette**
> **Crescent Rolls**
> **Grasshopper Parfaits**

STEAK DIANE

- 2 tablespoons butter or margarine
- ½ cup thinly sliced fresh mushrooms
- 1 teaspoon instant minced onion
- ½ teaspoon garlic salt
- ½ teaspoon lemon juice
- ½ teaspoon Worcestershire sauce
- 1 tablespoon snipped parsley or ½ teaspoon parsley flakes
- 2 tablespoons butter or margarine
- ½ pound beef tenderloin, cut into ¼-inch slices

Melt 2 tablespoons butter in 1-quart saucepan; cook and stir mushrooms, onion, garlic salt, lemon juice and Worcestershire sauce until mushrooms are tender. Stir in parsley; keep sauce warm.

Melt 2 tablespoons butter in 8-inch skillet; cook meat over medium-high heat, turning once, to medium doneness, 2 to 4 minutes on each side. To serve, spoon mushroom sauce onto meat. *2 servings*.

Note: A ¾-pound sirloin steak, ½ inch thick and with bone removed, can be substituted for the beef tenderloin. Pound sirloin steak to ¼-inch thickness and cut into 4 pieces.

Note: To flame sauce, warm 2 tablespoons brandy in attractive small pan. Ignite and pour onto meat.

POTATO SOUFFLÉ

Heat oven to 350°. Prepare instant mashed potato puffs as directed on package for 2 servings. Beat 2 egg whites and ½ teaspoon salt until soft peaks form. Beat 2 egg yolks; stir into hot potatoes. Fold potato mixture into egg whites. Pour into buttered 2½-cup casserole; sprinkle paprika on top. Bake until golden brown, about 30 minutes. *2 servings.*

TOMATOES VINAIGRETTE

Cut 2 tomatoes into ½-inch slices; arrange in single layer in glass dish. Sprinkle with salt and pepper. Top each tomato slice with 1 tablespoon sliced green onion and 1 teaspoon snipped parsley. Drizzle Clear French Dressing (below) on tomatoes. Cover and refrigerate 2 to 3 hours. Serve on lettuce and drizzle small amount of dressing on each serving. *2 servings.*

Clear French Dressing

½ cup salad oil
¼ cup vinegar
1 tablespoon sugar
1½ teaspoons salt
¼ teaspoon celery seed
¼ teaspoon dry mustard
¼ teaspoon grated onion or ⅛ teaspoon onion powder
1 small clove garlic

Mix all ingredients except garlic in tightly covered jar. Add garlic; let stand in dressing about 1 hour, then remove. *¾ cup.*

GRASSHOPPER PARFAITS

1 tablespoon white crème de cacao
1 tablespoon green crème de menthe
1 to 1½ cups vanilla ice cream

Mix crème de cacao and crème de menthe. Alternate layers of ice cream and 1 tablespoon liqueur mixture in each parfait glass. Place in freezer until serving time. *2 servings.*

Variation

Crème de Menthe Parfaits: Substitute 2 tablespoons crème de menthe syrup for the liqueur mixture.

Broiled Lobster Tails with Lemon Butter
Broccoli Spears
Lettuce Wedges with Cucumber-
Tomato Mayonnaise
Hot Rolls
Individual Lemon Schaum Tortes

BROILED LOBSTER TAILS

2 quarts water
2 tablespoons salt
2 frozen lobster tails (about 8 ounces each)
2 tablespoons butter or margarine, melted
  Lemon Butter (page 14)

In large saucepan, heat water and salt to boiling. Add frozen lobster tails; heat to boiling. Reduce heat; cover and simmer until done, about 12 minutes. Drain.

Cut down sides of lobster tails with kitchen scissors to remove thin undershell covering the meat. To prevent tails from curling, insert long metal skewer from meat side through tail to shell side, then back through shell and meat at opposite end.

Set oven control at broil and/or 550°. Place tails meat side up on rack in broiler pan; brush with butter. Broil with tops 3 inches from heat 2 to 3 minutes. Serve with Lemon Butter. *2 servings.*

LETTUCE WEDGES WITH CUCUMBER-TOMATO MAYONNAISE

½ cup mayonnaise or salad dressing
¼ cup drained chopped cucumber
¼ cup drained chopped tomato
 1 teaspoon finely chopped onion or ⅛ teaspoon onion
   powder
   Dash salt
   Lettuce wedges

Mix mayonnaise, cucumber, tomato, onion and salt. Serve on lettuce wedges. *2 servings.*

INDIVIDUAL LEMON SCHAUM TORTES

Meringue Shells (below)
¼ **cup sugar**
1 **tablespoon cornstarch**
⅛ **teaspoon salt**
¼ **cup water**
1 **egg yolk, slightly beaten**
½ **teaspoon grated lemon peel**
1 **tablespoon lemon juice**
1 **tablespoon butter or margarine**
⅓ **cup chilled whipping cream or ⅔ cup frozen
   whipped topping (thawed)**

Bake Meringue Shells. In small saucepan, mix sugar, cornstarch and salt. Stir water into sugar mixture. Cook over medium heat, stirring constantly, until mixture thickens and comes to a boil. Boil and stir 1 minute.

Stir at least half the hot mixture gradually into egg yolk; mix into hot mixture in pan. Boil and stir 1 minute. Remove from heat; stir in lemon peel, lemon juice and butter. Cool to room temperature. Spoon into Meringue Shells; cover with plastic wrap. Refrigerate at least 12 hours.

In chilled bowl, beat cream until stiff; spread on filling. Garnish tortes with shredded lemon peel. *2 servings.*

Meringue Shells

Heat oven to 275°. Cover baking sheet with heavy brown paper. In small mixer bowl, beat 1 egg white and ⅛ teaspoon cream of tartar until foamy. Beat in ¼ cup sugar, 1 tablespoon at a time; continue beating until stiff and glossy.

On paper-covered baking sheet, shape meringue into two 3½-inch circles with back of spoon, building up sides. Bake 45 minutes. Turn off oven; leave meringues in oven with door closed until cool, about 1½ hours. *2 shells.*

Sweet-and-Sour Pork
Fluffy White Rice
Chinese Pea Pods
Carrot Sticks
Cucumber Sticks
Melon Boats with Sherbet

SWEET-AND-SOUR PORK

     Salad oil
     Sweet-and-Sour Sauce (right)
½ cup all-purpose flour
¼ cup cornstarch
1 teaspoon salt
¼ teaspoon monosodium glutamate
½ teaspoon baking powder
½ cup water
1 teaspoon salad oil
½ pound pork tenderloin, cut into ¼-inch slices
1 medium green pepper, cut into 1-inch pieces
1 small onion, cut into 1-inch pieces
1½ cups hot cooked rice

Pour oil into electric skillet or large saucepan to depth of 1 to 1½ inches. Heat to 375°, or until 1-inch bread cube browns in 1 minute. While oil heats, prepare Sweet-and-Sour Sauce.

In small bowl, beat flour, cornstarch, salt, monosodium glutamate, baking powder, water and 1 teaspoon oil with rotary beater until smooth. Dip meat into batter with tongs; fry in hot oil, turning once, until golden brown, 6 to 8 minutes. Drain; keep warm.

Stir green pepper and onion into Sweet-and-Sour Sauce. Cover and simmer until vegetables are crisp-tender, about 5 minutes. Serve meat and sauce on rice. *2 servings.*

Sweet-and-Sour Sauce

¼ **cup brown sugar (packed)**
2 **tablespoons cornstarch**
1 **can (8 ounces) pineapple tidbits, drained (reserve syrup)**
¼ **cup vinegar**
2 **tablespoons catsup**

In 2-quart saucepan, mix sugar and cornstarch. Add enough water to reserved pineapple syrup to measure 1 cup. Stir syrup mixture, vinegar and catsup into cornstarch mixture. Cook, stirring constantly, until mixture thickens and boils. Stir in pineapple. Keep warm over very low heat.

MELON BOATS WITH SHERBET

Top wedges of chilled honeydew melon or cantaloupe with scoops of lemon or lime sherbet.

Note: Melon out of season? Use 1 package (12 ounces) frozen melon balls, partially thawed, instead.

SOMETHING TO KNOW ABOUT...

Use tongs to dip each piece of pork into the batter; fry each piece as you've battered it. The pork will be easier to slice thin if it's partially frozen.

Curried Beef and Peppers
Buttered Noodles
Lettuce Wedges with Oil-and-Vinegar Dressing
Quick Sesame Bread
Fruit Medley

CURRIED BEEF AND PEPPERS

½ to ¾ pound beef round steak
2 tablespoons salad oil
1 beef bouillon cube
1¼ cups water
1 teaspoon sugar, if desired
1 teaspoon curry powder
½ teaspoon salt
1 small green pepper, cut into 1-inch pieces
1 medium onion, cut into wedges
2 tablespoons cornstarch
2 tablespoons water
1 tomato, peeled and cut into wedges
Buttered noodles

Cut meat into ¾-inch pieces. Heat oil in 8-inch skillet; brown meat over medium heat, about 10 minutes. Drain off fat.

Add bouillon cube, 1¼ cups water, the sugar, curry powder and salt; heat to boiling, stirring occasionally. Reduce heat; cover and simmer until meat is tender, about 1 hour. (Add small amount water if necessary.)

Add green pepper and onion; cover and simmer until vegetables are crisp-tender, about 5 minutes. Mix cornstarch and 2 tablespoons water; stir into meat and vegetable mixture. Cook over medium heat, stirring constantly, until sauce is clear and bubbly, about 1 minute. Add tomato wedges; cover and cook over low heat until tomatoes are hot, about 3 minutes. Serve on noodles. *2 servings*.

QUICK SESAME BREAD

1 cup buttermilk baking mix
¼ cup water
2 teaspoons soft butter or margarine
1 tablespoon sesame seed

Heat oven to 400°. Stir baking mix and water with fork to a soft dough. On greased baking sheet, spread or roll dough into rectangle, 6x4 inches. Brush butter on rectangle; sprinkle with sesame seed. Bake until golden brown, 8 to 10 minutes. Serve hot, broken into pieces or cut into squares. *2 servings.*

FRUIT MEDLEY

Choose two or more of the following fruits to total 1 to 1½ cups: seedless green grapes; strawberries; banana slices; peach, pear or pineapple chunks; mandarin orange segments; dark sweet cherries. Divide between dessert dishes; sprinkle snipped fresh mint on fruit if desired. Serve with one of the toppings below. *2 servings.*

Honey-Yogurt Topping

Mix 1 tablespoon lemon juice, 1 tablespoon honey and ½ cup unflavored yogurt or dairy sour cream.

Brown Sugar-Yogurt Topping

Mix ¼ cup unflavored yogurt or dairy sour cream and 2 tablespoons brown sugar.

Limeade-Yogurt Topping

Mix 2 tablespoons frozen limeade concentrate (thawed) and ¼ cup pineapple yogurt.

Spice-Yogurt Topping

Mix ½ cup unflavored yogurt or dairy sour cream, 1 tablespoon sugar, ¼ teaspoon cinnamon and dash nutmeg.

```
┌─────────────────────────────────────────┐
│  ┌───────────────────────────────────┐  │
│  │                                   │  │
│  │           Coq au Vin              │  │
│  │       Tossed Romaine Salad        │  │
│  │        Crusty French Bread        │  │
│  │     Pots de Crème au Chocolat     │  │
│  │                                   │  │
│  └───────────────────────────────────┘  │
└─────────────────────────────────────────┘
```

COQ AU VIN

     3 slices bacon
    ¼ cup all-purpose flour
    ½ teaspoon salt
    ⅛ teaspoon pepper
  1½ pounds chicken pieces (legs, thighs, breasts)
    ¼ pound fresh mushrooms, sliced
     2 small onions, cut into halves
     2 carrots, cut diagonally into 2-inch pieces
     1 teaspoon instant chicken bouillon or 1 chicken
        bouillon cube
    ½ teaspoon Italian herb seasoning or ⅛ teaspoon each
        thyme, basil, marjoram and sage
    ¾ cup water
    ½ cup red Burgundy
        Snipped parsley

In Dutch oven or 3-quart saucepan, fry bacon until
crisp; remove and drain. Mix flour, salt and pepper in
plastic or paper bag. Shake chicken, 2 or 3 pieces at a
time, in bag until coated. Brown chicken in bacon fat;
remove to warm platter.

Cook and stir mushrooms and onion in Dutch oven
until onion is tender. Drain off fat. Place chicken in
Dutch oven; crumble bacon on chicken and add remaining ingredients except parsley. Heat to boiling.
Reduce heat; cover and simmer until thickest chicken
pieces are tender, about 30 minutes. Sprinkle parsley
on top. *2 servings.*

Time-saver: You can substitute canned vegetables for
the fresh. Use 1 jar (2 ounces) button mushrooms, 1

can (8¾ ounces) small onions and 1 can (8 ounces) whole carrots. Drain and reserve liquids. Add enough water to reserved vegetable liquids to measure ¾ cup. Substitute this liquid for the ¾ cup water. Add canned vegetables after chicken has simmered and is tender; heat through, about 10 minutes.

TOSSED ROMAINE SALAD

    3 cups bite-size pieces romaine (1 small head)
    4 or 5 radishes, sliced
    2 tablespoons salad oil
    1 tablespoon wine, tarragon or cider vinegar
    1 small clove garlic, crushed, or ⅛ teaspoon garlic
       powder
    ¼ teaspoon salt
       Dash pepper

Combine romaine and radish slices in bowl. Mix remaining ingredients; pour onto vegetables and toss. *2 servings.*

POTS DE CRÈME AU CHOCOLAT

    ½ bar (4-ounce size) sweet cooking chocolate
    1 tablespoon sugar
    ⅓ cup light cream (20%)
    1 egg yolk, slightly beaten
    ¼ teaspoon vanilla

In small saucepan, cook chocolate, sugar and cream over medium heat, stirring constantly, until chocolate is melted and mixture is smooth. Remove from heat; beat into egg yolk. Stir in vanilla. Pour into pots de crème cups, demitasse cups or other small dessert dishes. Chill. If you like, serve with whipped cream and garnish with mint leaf. *2 servings.*

Salted Almonds
Olives
Paella
Orange-Avocado Salad
Caramel Custard (page 62)
Sangría

PAELLA

   2 tablespoons salad oil
   1 to 1½ pounds chicken pieces
   1 small onion, sliced
   1 can (8 ounces) stewed tomatoes
   1 teaspoon salt
   1 teaspoon paprika
   ¼ teaspoon pepper
      Dash cayenne red pepper
   ½ package (6-ounce size) saffron rice (½ cup)
1½ cups chicken broth*
   1 can (4½ ounces) medium shrimp, rinsed and drained
   ½ package (10-ounce size) frozen green peas,
      broken apart (about 1 cup)

Heat oil in Dutch oven; brown chicken. Remove chicken and set aside. Drain off fat.

Heat oven to 350°. Cook and stir onion, tomatoes and seasonings in Dutch oven until onion is tender, about 5 minutes. Stir in rice and broth; heat to boiling. Add chicken. Cover and bake 35 minutes. Add shrimp and peas; bake until chicken is tender, about 10 minutes. Serve in paella pan or shallow serving dish. Garnish with pimiento strips, parsley and artichoke hearts. *2 servings.*

Note: Saffron rice hard to come by? You can substitute ½ cup uncooked regular rice plus a dash of saffron or ⅛ teaspoon turmeric.

*Chicken broth can be made by dissolving 1 chicken bouillon cube in 1½ cups boiling water, or use canned chicken broth.

ORANGE-AVOCADO SALAD

1 orange, pared and sliced
1 avocado, pared and cut into wedges
1 small onion, sliced and separated into rings
   Crisp salad greens
   Orange Dressing (below)

Arrange orange slices, avocado wedges and onion rings on salad greens. Drizzle Orange Dressing on salads. *2 servings*.

Orange Dressing

¼ cup salad oil
1 tablespoon lemon juice
½ teaspoon grated orange peel
2 tablespoons orange juice
1 tablespoon sugar
⅛ teaspoon salt
⅛ teaspoon dry mustard

Shake all ingredients in tightly covered jar. *½ cup*.

Note: Use leftover dressing for Orange-Cucumber Salad (page 95).

SOMETHING TO KNOW ABOUT . . .

At one time avocados seemed to be the private property of Californians—today we all get to share the wealth.

For best flavor, use only ripe avocados. (A ripe avocado will yield to gentle pressure when held between the palms of your hands.) If necessary, leave at room temperature for several days to ripen.

To use, cut the avocado lengthwise into halves. (Your knife will hit the large hard seed.) Twist gently to separate. To remove the seed easily, strike it with a sharp knife, twist the seed gently and lift it out. With a paring knife, carefully strip off the avocado skin. If the avocado will not be used immediately, drizzle the cut surfaces with lemon juice to prevent discoloration.

Duckling à l'Orange
Barley Pilaf
Mushroom Green Beans or Spinach Soufflé
Tomato-Endive Toss
Mocha Ice-cream Puffs

DUCKLING À L'ORANGE

    4- to 5-pound duckling
    2 tablespoons butter or margarine
    2 tablespoons finely chopped onion
    ¼ teaspoon tarragon leaves
    1½ tablespoons shredded orange peel
    ½ cup orange juice
    ¼ teaspoon salt
    ⅛ teaspoon dry mustard
    ¼ cup currant jelly
    2 tablespoons port or cranberry cocktail
    1 teaspoon cornstarch

Fasten neck skin of duckling with skewers. Lift wing
tips up and over back for natural brace. Heat oven to
325°. Place duckling breast side up on rack in shallow
roasting pan.

Melt butter in small saucepan. Cook and stir onion
and tarragon leaves in butter until onion is tender. Add
orange peel, orange juice, salt, mustard, jelly and port;
cook and stir over medium heat until jelly is melted.

Measure orange sauce; reserve half the sauce to
serve with duckling. Brush duckling with part of remaining orange sauce. Roast uncovered until done,
about 2½ hours, pricking skin with fork and brushing
occasionally with remaining orange sauce. If duckling
is browning too quickly, cover loosely with aluminum
foil. Duckling is done when drumstick meat feels very
soft when pressed.

In small saucepan, mix reserved orange sauce and

the cornstarch. Cook over medium heat, stirring constantly, until mixture boils. Boil and stir 1 minute. Serve sauce in small pitcher. Remove duckling to warm platter; garnish with watercress, orange twists, grapes or kumquats. *2 servings.*

SOMETHING TO KNOW ABOUT...

To serve the duckling after you've presented it at the table, cut it lengthwise in half. Keep close to the top of the wishbone and the center of the back. Then cut each half into 2 pieces. (Poultry shears work best for this, but you can also use kitchen shears or a sharp, sturdy knife.)

BARLEY PILAF

1 tablespoon butter or margarine
⅓ cup uncooked barley
1 tablespoon instant minced onion
1 teaspoon instant chicken bouillon
¼ teaspoon celery salt
⅛ teaspoon pepper
1 cup boiling water
1 tablespoon snipped parsley

Heat oven to 325°. In ungreased 2½-cup casserole, mix all ingredients except parsley. Cover and bake until done, about 1 hour. Stir in parsley. *2 servings.*

SPINACH SOUFFLÉ

Heat oven to 325°. Remove frozen spinach soufflé (12-ounce size) from container. Cut into quarters. Place 2 quarters in each of 2 ungreased 10-ounce baking dishes, overlapping quarters if necessary. Bake until knife inserted in center comes out clean, 50 to 60 minutes. *2 servings.*

MUSHROOM GREEN BEANS

1 can (2 ounces) mushroom stems and pieces, drained (reserve liquid)
½ package (10-ounce size) frozen French-style green beans*
¼ teaspoon salt
1 teaspoon butter or margarine

Add enough water to reserved mushroom liquid to measure ¼ cup; pour into small saucepan. Add beans and salt. Cover and cook until tender, about 5 minutes. Drain. Stir in butter and mushrooms; heat through. *2 servings.*

* **Leftover frozen green beans?** Use in Deep-dish Hamburger Pie (page 112).

TOMATO-ENDIVE TOSS

3 cups bite-size pieces endive
2 tomatoes, cut into wedges
   Clear French Dressing (page 187)
   Onion rings
   Marinated artichoke hearts, if desired

Toss endive, tomatoes and 3 tablespoons of the dressing. Garnish with onion rings and artichoke hearts. *2 servings.*

MOCHA ICE-CREAM PUFFS

½ cup water
¼ cup butter or margarine
½ cup all-purpose flour
 2 eggs
   Coffee ice cream
¼ cup chocolate syrup
 2 teaspoons orange-flavored liqueur, if desired

Heat oven to 400°. In 1-quart saucepan, heat water and butter to rolling boil. Stir in flour. Stir vigorously over low heat until mixture forms a ball, about 1 minute. Remove from heat. Beat in eggs, all at one time, until smooth. Drop dough by scant ¼ cupfuls 3 inches apart onto ungreased baking sheet (makes 6 puffs). Bake until puffed and golden, about 35 minutes. Cool.

Cut off tops of 2 cream puffs. Pull out any filaments of soft dough. Fill puffs with ice cream. Mix chocolate syrup and liqueur; drizzle on cream puffs. *2 puffs—and 4 more for other times.*

Note: Store the extra puffs unfilled and serve the following day or wrap in aluminum foil, label and freeze. To serve, fill with sweetened whipped cream, ice cream or pudding.

Broiled Sirloin Steak
Easy Hash Browns with Onions
Gourmet Tossed Salad
Warm Apple Pie (as below)

BROILED SIRLOIN STEAK

1- to 1½-pound beef sirloin steak, 1 to 1½ inches thick

Set oven control at broil and/or 550°. Diagonally slash outer edge of fat on steak at 1-inch intervals to prevent curling (do not cut into lean). Broil steak with top 3 to 5 inches from heat to desired doneness, 6 to 8 minutes on each side for rare, 8 to 10 minutes for medium. Test for doneness by cutting a small slit near center of meat. Season steak *after* browning. (Salt tends to draw moisture to surface and delay browning.) Serve immediately. *2 servings.*

Note: Use this method for broiling top loin, porterhouse, T-bone, rib or rib eye steaks.

EASY HASH BROWNS WITH ONIONS

½ **package (5.5-ounce size) hash brown potatoes with onions***
⅔ **cup water**
½ **teaspoon salt**
 2 **tablespoons butter or margarine**

In 8-inch skillet, combine half the potatoes, the water, salt and butter. Cook uncovered over medium-high heat until liquid is absorbed and potatoes are brown on bottom, 8 to 10 minutes. Turn with pancake turner and cook until brown on bottom, about 3 minutes. *2 servings.*

* To use half the package, measure contents and divide in half (approximately 1 cup). To store remaining mix,

close package securely and use within 2 weeks. Serve again with scrambled eggs, chops or broiled chicken.

GOURMET TOSSED SALAD

2½ cups bite-size pieces crisp salad greens
½ cup sliced fresh mushrooms
½ cup small cauliflowerets
2 tablespoons chopped green pepper
1 to 2 tablespoons crumbled blue cheese
   Oil-and-Vinegar Dressing (page 58)
   Thinly sliced onion rings
   Pimiento-stuffed olive slices

Toss salad greens, mushrooms, cauliflowerets, green pepper, cheese and dressing in bowl. Garnish with onion rings and olive slices. *2 servings.*

WARM APPLE PIE

   Pastry for 8-inch two-crust pie (page 204)
½ cup sugar
3 tablespoons flour
¼ teaspoon nutmeg
¼ teaspoon cinnamon
   Dash salt
5 cups thinly sliced pared tart apples (about 5 medium)
1 tablespoon butter or margarine

Prepare pastry. Mix sugar, flour, nutmeg, cinnamon and salt; pour on apples and toss. Turn filling into pastry-lined pie pan and dot with butter.

Heat oven to 425°. Cover filling with top crust which has slits cut in it; seal and flute. Cover edge with 2- to 3-inch-wide strip of aluminum foil to prevent excessive browning; remove foil last 15 minutes of baking. Bake until crust is golden brown and juice begins to bubble through crust, 40 to 50 minutes. Cool slightly on wire rack. Serve warm, with cinnamon ice cream or Cheddar cheese if you like.

SOMETHING SPECIAL...

Pastry for Pies

Into mixing bowl, measure **1½ cups all-purpose flour** and **¾ teaspoon salt** (if using self-rising flour, omit salt). Cut in **½ cup plus 2 tablespoons shortening.** Sprinkle in **3 tablespoons water** gradually, mixing with fork until all flour is moistened. Shape dough firmly into ball. Divide dough in half; shape one half into flattened round on lightly floured cloth-covered board.

Roll dough 1½ inches larger all around than pie

Cut shortening into flour with pastry blender, using a rocking motion, until mixture looks like coarse crumbs.

Shape dough firmly into a ball when all flour is moistened and dough leaves side of bowl almost clean.

Roll with light strokes from the center outward, lifting rolling pin as you reach edge so dough does not become too thin.

pan, using stockinet-covered rolling pin. Carefully lift dough occasionally; if it sticks, rub a little flour into cloth beneath and continue rolling. Ease pastry into 8-inch pie pan. Turn filling into pan. Trim overhanging edge of pastry ½ inch from rim of pan with kitchen scissors. Shape remaining half of dough into flattened round and roll 2 inches larger all around than pie pan.

Cut slits in pastry; place on filling. Trim overhanging edge of pastry 1 inch from rim of pan. Fold and roll top edge of pastry under lower edge, pressing on rim to seal; flute. Cover edge of crust with 2- to 3-inch-wide strip of aluminum foil to prevent excessive browning during baking; remove foil for last 15 minutes of baking. Bake pie as directed in recipe.

Roll dough into circle 1½ inches larger all around than inverted pie pan, then fold into quarters, place in pan, unfold and ease in.

Fold pastry into quarters; cut 4 slits in each fold to allow steam to escape during baking. Place pastry on filling and unfold.

Fold and roll top edge of crust under lower edge. Flute; for a more definitive shape, repinch around handle of knife.

> **Breaded Veal Cutlets**
> **Quick Noodles Romanoff**
> **Zucchini Provençale**
> **Spumoni Ice-cream Bombe**

BREADED VEAL CUTLETS

  2 **veal cutlets (4 ounces each) or ½- to ¾-pound**
    boneless veal round steak, ½ inch thick
    Salt and pepper
  2 **tablespoons flour**
  1 **egg, slightly beaten**
  ¼ **cup dry bread crumbs**
  2 **tablespoons salad oil**
  ¼ **cup water**
    Lemon wedges

If using veal round steak, cut into 2 pieces. Sprinkle
meat with salt and pepper, then coat with flour. Dip
into egg, then coat with bread crumbs.

  Heat oil in 8-inch skillet; brown meat over medium
heat. Drain off fat. Add water and heat to boiling. Reduce heat; cover and simmer until done, about 30 minutes. (Add small amount of water if necessary.) Serve
with lemon wedges and garnish with parsley and olives.
2 servings.

QUICK NOODLES ROMANOFF

Measure contents of 1 package (5.5 ounces) noodles
Romanoff; divide in half (approximately 1 cup noodles
and ¼ cup Sour Cream-Cheese Sauce Mix).* Cook
half the noodles in 3 cups boiling salted water until
tender, 7 to 8 minutes. Drain noodles and return to
saucepan. Stir in 1 tablespoon butter or margarine, ¼
cup milk and ¼ cup Sour Cream-Cheese Sauce Mix.
Sprinkle paprika on top. *2 servings.*

* To store remaining mix, close package securely and

use within 2 weeks. Delicious with hamburgers, meat-balls or frankfurters.

ZUCCHINI PROVENCALE

1 medium zucchini
1 small onion, thinly sliced
¼ cup chopped green pepper
1 tablespoon salad oil
⅛ teaspoon instant minced garlic
½ teaspoon salt
  Dash pepper
1 tomato, peeled and cut into wedges
  Snipped parsley

Remove stem and blossom ends of zucchini but do not pare. Cut into ¼-inch slices. In 8-inch skillet, cook and stir all ingredients except tomato and parsley until hot. Cover and cook over medium heat, stirring occasionally, until vegetables are crisp-tender, about 5 minutes. Stir in tomato wedges; cover and cook until hot, 3 to 5 minutes. Sprinkle parsley on top. *2 servings.*

SPUMONI ICE-CREAM BOMBE

1 cup chocolate ice cream
1 cup spumoni ice cream

Soften chocolate ice cream slightly; spoon into chilled 1¾- to 2-cup mold or bowl and press on bottom and side of mold. Freeze until firm, about 1 hour.

Soften spumoni ice cream slightly; spoon into mold and press. Cover mold with aluminum foil and freeze until firm.

To unmold, turn mold onto chilled serving plate. Dip a cloth into hot water; wring out and place on mold for a minute or two. Lift off mold. If mold doesn't slip off easily, reapply hot cloth. Return bombe to freezer until serving time. Decorate with pressurized cream if desired. *2 generous servings.*

Note: Spumoni ice cream hard to find? Substitute pistachio or cherry or use orange sherbet.

Roast Cornish Hens
Wild Rice with Mushrooms and Almonds
Artichokes with Lemon Butter
Crescent Rolls
Pots de Crème au Chocolat (page 195)

ROAST CORNISH HENS

2 **Rock Cornish hens (about 1 pound each)**
Salt
¼ **cup soft butter or margarine**
¼ **teaspoon red pepper sauce or ½ teaspoon thyme,**
marjoram or tarragon leaves
Preserved kumquats
Watercress

Thaw hens if frozen. Heat oven to 350°. Rub cavities
of hens with salt if desired. Place hens breast side up on
rack in shallow roasting pan. Mix butter and red pepper sauce. Brush part of butter mixture on hens and
sprinkle with salt. Roast uncovered until tender, about
1 hour, brushing hens 3 or 4 times with remaining
butter mixture. Garnish with preserved kumquats and
watercress. *2 servings.*

WILD RICE WITH
MUSHROOMS AND ALMONDS

2 **tablespoons butter or margarine**
⅓ **cup uncooked wild rice**
1 **tablespoon slivered almonds**
1 **tablespoon chopped onion**
1 **can (2 ounces) mushroom stems and pieces**
1 **cup chicken broth***

Melt butter in 8-inch skillet; cook and stir rice, almonds
and onion until almonds are golden brown, about 10
minutes.

Heat oven to 350°. Stir mushrooms (with liquid) and chicken broth into skillet; heat to boiling. Pour rice mixture into ungreased 2½-cup casserole. Cover and bake until all liquid is absorbed and rice is tender, about 1 hour. *2 servings.*

*Chicken broth can be made by dissolving 1 chicken bouillon cube or 1 teaspoon instant chicken bouillon in 1 cup boiling water.

ARTICHOKES WITH LEMON BUTTER

1½ **quarts water**
  1 **tablespoon lemon juice**
½ **teaspoon salt**
  2 **artichokes**
     Lemon Butter (below)

In 3-quart saucepan, heat water, lemon juice and salt to boiling. Remove discolored leaves and the small leaves at base of each artichoke. Trim stem even with base of artichoke. Cut 1 inch off top and discard top. Snip off points of remaining leaves with scissors. Tie each artichoke with string around side and from top to bottom to hold leaves in place. Place artichokes in saucepan; heat to boiling.

Reduce heat; cover and simmer until done, 30 to 40 minutes. (Artichokes are done when leaves pull off easily and bottom is tender when pierced with knife.) Remove artichokes with tongs or 2 large spoons; place upside down to drain. Remove string and serve upright. Serve hot with Lemon Butter. *2 servings.*

Lemon Butter

Heat ¼ cup butter or margarine, 1 teaspoon grated lemon peel and 2 tablespoons lemon juice over low heat until butter is melted. *About ⅓ cup.*

Note: To eat artichokes, pull off leaves one at a time. Dip base of leaf into Lemon Butter; turn leaf meaty side down and draw between teeth, scraping off meat portion. Discard leaf on plate. When all leaves have been removed, cut off the spiny choke and eat the smooth round bottom portion—a great delicacy.

> **Oriental Fondue**
> **Fluffy White Rice**
> **Kumquats**
> **Almond Cookies**
> **Tea**

ORIENTAL FONDUE

Choose one to three of the following meats and seafoods to total ¾ pound:

> **Pork tenderloin, cut into ⅛-inch slices**
> **Chicken breasts, boned and cut across grain into bite-size slices (about ¼ inch thick)**
> **Frozen scallops, thawed and cut into ¾-inch pieces**
> **Cleaned raw shrimp, fresh or frozen***

Choose three or four of the following vegetables:

> **¼ cauliflower, separated into flowerets**
> **¼ pound broccoli, separated into flowerets**
> **½ package (10-ounce size) frozen Chinese pea pods**
> **2 medium carrots, cut diagonally into ⅛-inch slices**
> **¼ pound fresh mushrooms, thinly sliced**
> **1 bunch green onions (about 6), cut into ½-inch lengths**

And have ready:

> **8 cups chicken broth****
> **1½ cups hot cooked rice**
> **Choice of dipping sauces (right)**

Arrange meat, seafood and vegetables on tray or platter; garnish with parsley. Cover and refrigerate until serving time.

Pour chicken broth into 10-inch electric skillet, metal fondue pot or chafing dish until about ⅔ full (add any remaining chicken broth as needed); heat to simmering. Divide rice between 2 small bowls. Serve dipping sauces in small bowls.

Each person uses chopsticks or fondue forks to place an assortment of meat and vegetables (2 or 3 pieces at a time) in broth. Cook foods until done, 2 to 4 minutes; transfer to dinner plate and dip into a sauce. After the main course, ladle broth on remaining rice in bowls and eat as soup. *2 servings*.

Note: Meat will slice easier if partially frozen.

*Rinse frozen shrimp under running cold water to remove ice glaze.
**4 cans (13¾ ounces each) chicken broth and 1 cup water or 3 cans (10½ ounces each) condensed chicken broth, diluted as directed.

Lemon-Soy Sauce

¼ cup lemon juice
¼ cup soy sauce
2 tablespoons sweet sake (for cooking) or sherry

Mix all ingredients. *About ½ cup.*

Sweet-and-Sour Sauce

2 tablespoons brown sugar
1 teaspoon cornstarch
2 tablespoons cider vinegar
⅓ cup pineapple juice
1 tablespoon catsup

Mix all ingredients in small saucepan. Cook over medium-high heat, stirring constantly, until mixture thickens and boils. Boil and stir 1 minute. *About ½ cup.*

Plum Sauce

¼ cup chili sauce
¼ cup plum jam or grape jelly
¼ teaspoon hot sauce

Mix all ingredients. *About ½ cup.*

Hot Mustard Sauce

3 tablespoons dry mustard
2 tablespoons water

Mix ingredients. *About ¼ cup.*

> **Shrimp Curry and Condiments**
> **Green Rice**
> **Sesame Crackers**
> **Baked Banana (see below)**
> **Spiced Tea**

SHRIMP CURRY

    Condiments (below)
  1 can (10½ ounces) condensed cream of shrimp soup
  1 teaspoon parsley flakes
  ¾ teaspoon curry powder
  1 tablespoon instant minced onion
 12 ounces frozen cleaned raw shrimp*
    Green Rice (right)

Prepare Condiments. In medium saucepan, heat soup, parsley flakes, curry powder and onion to boiling, stirring occasionally. Stir in shrimp; heat to boiling. Reduce heat; cover and simmer until shrimp are done, about 10 minutes. Serve curry with Green Rice. *2 servings.*

*Rinse frozen shrimp under running cold water to remove ice glaze.

Condiments

Choose three to six of the following:

Diced tomatoes
Golden raisins   Chopped green pepper
Toasted shredded coconut   Grated orange peel
Chopped hard-cooked eggs   Grated lemon peel
Sweet pickle sticks   Salted diced almonds
Chutney   Currant jelly
Kumquats   Peeled and sliced avocado

GREEN RICE

⅔ cup uncooked regular rice
½ cup chopped fresh spinach leaves
2 teaspoons instant minced onion
1 tablespoon butter or margarine
1 teaspoon salt
1⅓ cups boiling water

Heat oven to 350°. Mix all ingredients in ungreased 1-quart casserole. Cover and bake until liquid is absorbed and rice is tender, about 30 minutes. *2 servings.*

BAKED BANANA

Heat oven to 350°. Cut peeled large banana lengthwise in half. Place halves cut sides down in greased baking dish and brush with lemon juice.

Drizzle with 1 tablespoon butter or margarine, melted, and if desired, 2 teaspoons light rum or ¼ teaspoon rum flavoring. Sprinkle 1 teaspoon grated lemon peel and 2 teaspoons brown sugar on top. Bake uncovered 20 minutes. Serve warm with butter pecan ice cream or any favorite flavor. *2 servings.*

SPICED TEA

2 tea bags
3 whole cloves, broken into pieces
¼ teaspoon dried orange peel
⅛ teaspoon cinnamon
2 cups boiling water

In heated teapot or other heatproof container, place tea bags, cloves, orange peel and cinnamon. Pour boiling water into teapot. Cover and steep 3 to 5 minutes. Stir just before serving. *2 servings.*

```
┌─────────────────────────────────────────┐
│  ┌───────────────────────────────────┐  │
│  │                                   │  │
│  │          Beef Fondue              │  │
│  │  Fresh Mushroom-Romaine Salad     │  │
│  │          French Bread             │  │
│  │          Velvet Frost             │  │
│  │                                   │  │
│  └───────────────────────────────────┘  │
└─────────────────────────────────────────┘
```

BEEF FONDUE

Trim fat from 1 pound beef tenderloin, tenderloin tips or boneless beef sirloin; cut meat into bite-size pieces (¾- to 1-inch cubes). Cover and refrigerate. Prepare sauces below or use commercially prepared sauces such as barbecue, horseradish and mustard.

About 15 minutes before dinner, mound pieces of meat on bed of greens. Pour salad oil into metal fondue pot to depth of 1 to 1½ inches. Heat on fondue stand over burner or on range to 375°, or until 1-inch bread cube browns in 1 minute.

Each person spears cube of meat with long-handled fork and cooks it in hot oil until crusty on outside and juicy and rare inside. Since the fork will be very hot by this time, meat should be transferred to a dinner fork and then dipped into a sauce. *2 servings.*

Garlic Butter Sauce

Beat ¼ cup soft butter or margarine until fluffy. Stir in 1 teaspoon snipped parsley and ⅛ teaspoon garlic powder. Refrigerate. Let come to room temperature before serving. *¼ cup.*

Blue Cheese Sauce

Combine ¼ cup dairy sour cream, 2 tablespoons crumbled blue cheese, ½ teaspoon Worcestershire sauce and ⅛ teaspoon salt. Refrigerate. *⅓ cup.*

Zesty Tomato Sauce

Mix ¼ cup catsup or chili sauce, 1 tablespoon lemon juice and 1 to 1½ teaspoons horseradish. *¼ cup.*

FRESH MUSHROOM-ROMAINE SALAD

¼ **pound fresh mushrooms, sliced**
 3 **cups bite-size pieces romaine**
   Herb Dressing (below)

Toss mushrooms, romaine and dressing in bowl. *2 servings.*

Herb Dressing

 2 **tablespoons lemon juice or vinegar**
½ **teaspoon sugar**
¼ **teaspoon salt**
¼ **teaspoon paprika**
¼ **teaspoon marjoram, basil or oregano**
½ **teaspoon Worcestershire sauce**
 1 **tablespoon salad oil**
 1 **clove garlic, crushed, or ⅛ teaspoon garlic powder**

Shake all ingredients in tightly covered jar. *About ¼ cup.*

VELVET FROST

1 **pint vanilla ice cream, softened**
2 **tablespoons white crème de cacao**
2 **tablespoons orange-flavored liqueur**

In blender or small mixer bowl, mix all ingredients until smooth. Divide between glasses or dessert cups. Garnish with whipped topping and stemmed maraschino cherries. Serve with straws and spoons. *2 servings.*

Variations

Brandy Alexander Frost: Substitute 2 tablespoons brandy for the orange-flavored liqueur.
Irish Coffee Frost: Omit crème de cacao and orange-flavored liqueur and add 2 tablespoons Irish whiskey and 2 teaspoons powdered instant coffee.

BONUS MAIN DISHES

CHICKEN BREASTS BAKED IN CREAM

  2 tablespoons butter or margarine
  1 to 1½ pounds chicken breasts
  1 tablespoon butter or margarine
  1 teaspoon flour
  ¼ cup finely chopped onion
  ½ teaspoon salt
  ⅛ teaspoon pepper
  ½ cup light cream (20%)
  ½ cup water
  ½ teaspoon instant chicken bouillon
  2 teaspoons Worcestershire sauce

Heat oven to 350°. In oven, melt 2 tablespoons butter
in baking pan, 9x9x2 inches. Place chicken in pan,
turning to coat with butter, and arrange skin side up.
Bake uncovered 1 hour.

Melt 1 tablespoon butter in small saucepan. Stir in
flour, onion, salt and pepper. Cook over low heat, stirring constantly, until mixture is bubbly and onion is
tender. Remove from heat; stir in cream, water,
bouillon and Worcestershire sauce. Heat to boiling,
stirring constantly. Boil and stir 1 minute.

Remove chicken from oven; drain off fat. Pour sauce
on chicken; cover and bake 15 minutes. *2 servings.*

An ensemble of Wild Rice with Mushrooms and
Almonds (page 208), buttered peas, Stuffed Pear Salad
(page 23) and Pots de Crème au Chocolat (page 195)
adds just the right touch of elegance.

HAM WELLINGTON

  1 stick or ½ packet pie crust mix
1½- pound canned ham
  1 egg yolk, slightly beaten
  ¼ cup chutney or apricot preserves

Heat oven to 425°. Grease baking pan, 9x9x2 inches.
Prepare pastry for One-crust Pie as directed on pack-

age except—roll dough into rectangle, 12x8 inches. Trim edges to make even; reserve excess pastry.

Remove gelatin from ham. Place ham in center of rectangle. Overlap pastry to cover ham, moistening edges and ends with water to seal securely. Place seam side down in pan. Brush egg yolk on pastry. Roll left-over dough 1/8 to 1/16 inch thick. Cut into petal shapes and arrange in a flower design on top of ham. (Or make a design of your own choosing.) Bake until golden brown, about 30 minutes. Heat chutney in small saucepan; serve with ham. *2 servings*.

Perfect with baked sweet potatoes and Brussels Sprouts with Cashews (page 20). Want a distinctive dessert? How about Peaches Flambé (page 175)?

Note: What about the egg white? Store in covered small container in refrigerator up to 3 days. Can be used for Individual Brownie Alaskas (page 7) or Meringue Shells (page 189)—fill shells with ice cream or fruit.

VEAL SCALOPPINE

> 2 boneless veal cutlets (about 4 ounces each) or
> ¾-pound veal round steak, ½ inch thick
> Salt and pepper
> ¼ cup all-purpose flour
> 2 tablespoons butter or margarine
> 1 can (2 ounces) mushroom stems and pieces
> ¼ cup white wine or apple juice
> ¼ cup water
> 1 teaspoon instant beef bouillon or 1 beef bouillon cube
> ½ teaspoon parsley flakes

If using round steak, pound meat until ¼ inch thick; cut into 2 pieces. Season with salt and pepper, then coat with flour. Melt butter in 8-inch skillet; brown meat, 3 to 4 minutes on each side. Stir in remaining ingredients; heat to boiling, stirring occasionally. Reduce heat; cover and simmer until tender, about 30 minutes. Serve meat with sauce. *2 servings*.

Hot cooked noodles, broccoli spears with lemon butter and Tomatoes Vinaigrette (page 187) complete the Italian mood. Try Mocha Ice-cream Puffs (page 200) for the grand finale.

BOILED LOBSTER

3 quarts water
3 tablespoons salt
2 live lobsters (1¼ pounds each)

In large kettle, heat water and salt to boiling. Plunge live lobsters headfirst into water. Cover and heat to boiling. Reduce heat; simmer about 10 minutes. Drain.

Place lobster on its back. Cut lengthwise in half with sharp knife. Remove the stomach, which is just in back of the head, and the intestinal vein, which runs from the stomach to the tip of the tail. Do not discard the green liver and coral roe; they're tasty. Crack claws. *2 servings.*

Serve with lemon wedges and melted butter, baked potatoes, tossed green salad, raspberry sherbet and white wine.

FISH AU GRATIN

1 package (12 ounces) frozen halibut steaks
½ teaspoon salt
¼ teaspoon oregano leaves
1 green onion, finely chopped
1½ teaspoons dry bread crumbs
1 tablespoon grated Parmesan cheese
1 tablespoon butter or margarine, melted
½ cup Sauterne or chicken broth

Heat oven to 400°. Place frozen fish in ungreased baking dish, 9x9x2 inches. Sprinkle with salt and oregano. Mix onions, bread crumbs, cheese and butter; spread on fish. Pour Sauterne into baking dish. Bake uncovered until fish flakes easily with fork, about 30 minutes. *2 servings.*

Try this with buttered asparagus spears, Tomatoes Vinaigrette (page 187), hot rolls and Individual Lemon Schaum Tortes (page 189).

BASIC KNOW-HOW

Just-for-two tips on shopping, storing and kitchen coping

WHAT EVERY KITCHEN FOR TWO NEEDS

FOR MEASURING

Measuring spoons (2 sets)
Set of nested dry
   measuring cups

Liquid measuring cups
   (1-cup, 1-quart)
Flexible metal spatula

FOR PREPARATION

Set of mixing bowls
Wooden spoons
Metal spoons
Rubber scrapers (wide and
   narrow)
Cutting board
French knife
Bread knife
2 paring knives
Utility knife (long,
   narrow-handled)
Can opener
Bottle and jar opener
Long-handled fork
Pancake turner
Slotted spoon
Tongs
Kitchen scissors

Vegetable parer
Vegetable brush
Pastry brush
Skewers
Grater (4-sided
   combined grater and
   shredder)
Pepper mill
Strainer
Colander
Electric mixer
Rotary beater
Toaster
Rolling pin and cover
Pastry cloth
Pastry blender
Kitchen timer

FOR BAKING

Casseroles (20-ounce,
   1-quart, 2-quart)
Dutch oven

Baking sheet (without
   sides)
2 round layer pans (9x1½)

Individual baking dishes (at least 2)

6 custard cups (6-ounce size)

2 custard cups (10-ounce size)

Baking pan (8x8x2 or 9x9x2)

Loaf pan (9x5x3)

Small roasting pan (with rack)

Muffin pan

Pie pan (8-inch)

Wire cooling rack

Pot holders

Meat thermometer

FOR TOP-OF-THE-RANGE COOKING

Covered skillets (8-inch, 10-inch)

Covered saucepans (1-quart, 2-quart, 3-quart or Dutch oven)

SERVING PIECES

Soufflé dish

Pizza pan and pizza cutter

Chafing dish

Fondue pot and accessories

Ovenproof skillet

Ramekins

Electric hot tray

Small dessert dishes

Parfait glasses

Individual salad bowls

NICE TO HAVE

Teakettle

Coffee maker

Teapot

Double boiler

Hibachi

Griddle

Omelet pan

Tube pan

Baking pan (13x9x2)

Jelly roll pan (15½x10½x1)

Individual loaf pans (4½x2½x1½)

Electric blender

Electric skillet

Toaster-oven

Food chopper or grinder

Knife sharpener

Carving knife

Gelatin molds (individual and 4-cup size)

Ladle

Wire whip

Baster

Poultry shears

Mallet

Funnel

Juicer

Ice-cream scoop

Cheese slicer

Biscuit cutter (2-inch or set of rounds)

Melon ball cutter

Apple corer

Candy and deep fat thermometer

Salt and pepper set for range

Canister set

Cake safe

Bread box

Lettuce crisper

Utility tray

Refrigerator containers

MARKETING

To be a good cook, you should be a successful shopper. After all, a menu is only as good as the foods that go into it. Here, then, are a few tips to improve your marketing know-how.

☐ Try to plan for the week ahead. Use the "specials" advertised in the newspaper as your guide to good buys.

☐ Meat will be your principal purchase. So decide on that first. Then fit the other pieces of your menu jigsaw around it.

☐ Shop with a list, but allow for flexibility. A good price on pork or fresh-picked corn is well worth a change of plans.

☐ Keep a pad in the kitchen and note any dwindling staple items—before you run out completely.

☐ Learn to list items as they're arranged in the store. Why waste time dashing back and forth?

☐ If possible, do your shopping when the store is least apt to be crowded. Avoid cart clashes, checkout-line waits, unnecessary wear and tear.

☐ Buy only what you can use—or store easily. That "two for" bargain is apt to turn into "one for" throwing out. Admittedly it's hard to hold back when potatoes are cheaper by the 10-pound sack, but resist you must, unless you're partial to sprouted Idahoes. And even the most stable of staples is better small—and more often. Nothing keeps forever!

☐ Look at the lists of have-on-hands below and take it from there. Only by experience will you learn which foods are important for *you* to keep in stock and which ones *you* can happily live without.

STAPLES

Flour
Buttermilk baking mix
Cornmeal
Cornstarch
Sugar: granulated, brown, confectioners'
Salt and pepper
Shortening

Vanilla
Lemon, almond, mint and sherry extracts
Worcestershire sauce
Red pepper sauce
Instant beef and chicken bouillon or bouillon cubes

Salad oil
Rice
Sphaghetti, macaroni and
 noodles
Salad dressings
Vinegar
Bottled lemon juice
Baking powder
Baking soda
Cream of tartar

Instant minced onion
Instant minced garlic or
 garlic powder
Parsley flakes
Mustard and catsup
Pickles and olives
Jams and jellies
Coffee and tea
Herbs and spices

FROZEN FOODS

Cubed steaks, chicken
 pieces, shrimp, crabmeat,
 fish fillets, fish sticks
Main dishes
Potatoes—French fried,
 patties
Vegetables and fruits

Desserts—pound cake,
 waffles, ice cream,
 sherbet, individual pies,
 tart shells, whipped
 topping
Fruit juices

CANNED FOODS

Ham, beef stew, chicken,
 tuna, salmon, luncheon
 meat, shrimp
Soups—an assortment
Fruits and vegetables
Relishes
Evaporated and
 condensed milk

Miscellaneous—ready-to-
 serve sauces, ready-to-
 serve puddings, fruit pie
 fillings, ready-to-spread
 frostings, toppings

PACKAGED FOODS

Soup, sauce and gravy
 mixes
Salad dressing mixes
Flavored gelatins
Cake mixes—several
 flavors
Dessert mixes and
 toppings
Muffin mixes
Pie crust mix
Casserole mixes—scalloped
 and au gratin potatoes

Rice and noodle mixes
Instant mashed potato
 puffs
Instant nonfat dry milk
Herbed croutons
Dry bread crumbs
Soda crackers
Graham crackers and/or
 crumbs
Breakfast cereals
Grated Parmesan cheese

MEAT

Since meat takes the biggest bite out of your food budget, it pays to get the most value and good solid nutrition for your money. That's not always easy. What appears to be a juicy steak at the meat counter may turn out to be an expensive mis-steak at your table. Inescapable conclusion: It's important to be a smart meat shopper.

How to Buy

Look before you buy. Look for flecks of fat within the lean as your clue to the meat's juiciness, flavor and tenderness. Lean meat that is bright colored, firm and fine textured denotes high quality. Look, too, for an official indication of quality.

Except for fresh pork, almost all meat is inspected and graded by the United States Department of Agriculture. The round federal inspection stamp or the USDA shield assures you that the meat is tableworthy. Grades of meat are identified on the USDA shield as "Prime," "Choice" or "Good." There *are* lesser grades, but you aren't likely to encounter them at the store. On the other hand, you won't find much "Prime" either—most of this is bought by restaurants.

A package of meat that doesn't carry either the stamp or the shield isn't necessarily a reject. Uncle Sam's seal of approval may have been marked on a part of the animal which was trimmed away. Or if you're buying something like liver or ground beef, you won't find a label at all. And in the case of veal, although it *is* graded, it's more likely to carry a label that says something like "Milk-Fed Veal," which doesn't really indicate how high up in the veal echelon that package of meat belongs.

Actually, aside from being aware of meat grades, another good way to shop for meat is to find a patient, knowledgeable meat man who will tell you what you need to know and whose wares haven't disappointed you. Even in the largest supermarket there is usually someone to guide you through the complexities of animal anatomy.

A final word on meat selection: Don't equate cost

with nutrition! Budget cuts have as much protein value as their higher-priced cousins. Just cook them right and they'll be flavorful, delicious *and* tender. The USDA grades indicate quality, not nutritional value.

How Much to Buy

Here's an answer you may not think very helpful: "It all depends." On the face of it, that's hardly definitive. On the other hand, you can take comfort in the fact that in buying meat, there's plenty of room to move around. The "all depends" are these:

☐ How much actual *meat* (versus bone and fat) you'll get to the pound. (A pound of ground beef will obviously go quite a bit farther than a pound of spareribs will.)

☐ How old, how active and how hungry the eaters are.

☐ How much time you have for fixing and how much space for storing.

☐ How good a buy you can get. It may be worthwhile to buy a turkey or large roast and plan to use it for several meals (see pages 140–171).

HOW MUCH TO BUY?

BONELESS CUTS (such as ground meat, stew meat, tenderloin)	¼ to ⅓ lb. per serving
BONELESS ROASTS (such as rolled beef, pork shoulder, beef tip)	⅓ to ½ lb. per serving
MEDIUM BONE IN (such as pot roast, country-style ribs)	½ to ¾ lb. per serving
LARGE BONE IN (such as shanks, short ribs, spareribs)	¾ to 1 lb. per serving

How to Store

In the refrigerator: As with all perishables, the watchword is *speed*. The shorter the time lapse between the meat counter and your refrigerator, the less chance there will be of the meat losing flavor or spoiling. To be at its best, use fresh meat within 2 or 3 days, ground beef and variety meats (liver, tongue and so forth) within 24 hours. There's no harm in keeping meat in its store wrap for a day or two, but it's a good idea to loosen the ends of the package to let air reach the meat. The object of this maneuver is to dry the surface of the meat ever so slightly; this seals in the juices and also slows the growth of bacteria.

Cured and smoked meats, sausages and sandwich meats are best refrigerated in their original packages until opened. Then bundle the leftovers in a plastic bag or tight wrapping. A cured ham (in its original wrap) can be stored in the refrigerator up to 2 weeks. Most canned hams should be stored in the refrigerator. If unopened, they can be kept safely up to 6 months.

Leftover cooked meat? Same treatment. Cool quickly; cover and refrigerate promptly. Finish up in 1 or 2 days . . . or wrap tightly and freeze; the time limits are:
- [ ] Plain—1 month
- [ ] With broth or gravy—6 months

In the freezer: If you plan to freeze meat, do it as soon after shopping as possible—because the quality you put in is the quality you'll take out.

Just about all meats freeze well and maintain their quality if wrapped properly, frozen quickly and stored at a temperature of 0° or below. Be sure to use a moisture-vapor-proof wrap such as heavy-duty aluminum foil, heavily waxed freezer paper or specially laminated paper. Wrap the meat tightly—the intent here is to eliminate as much air as possible from within the package. An improperly wrapped package can spell disaster. If air gets in, it will draw moisture from the meat and the meat will become dry, less flavorful and show indications of freezer burn (discoloration).

Meat bought already frozen can go from the store's freezer to yours "as is," but don't forget to mark it with the date. (Make sure the meat cut and its weight are also noted.) You can also freeze *fresh* meat in the transparent wrap it comes in—providing you plan to use it within a week or two. For longer storage, tuck the original package into a heavyweight plastic bag, or overwrap with any sturdy freezer material. Press all the air out of the package before sealing.

To conserve freezer space and save time later, you may want to get your meat ready for the pan before freezing. Trim off excess fat; divide meat into portions; form ground beef into patties; separate chops, small steaks and patties with a double thickness of aluminum foil or waxed paper. Such do-aheads will make life easier for you at the thawing end. The only thing you *don't* want to do is season meat beforehand, as salt shortens freezer life.

HOW LONG TO STORE?
(For best quality, consider these periods maximum.)

	DAYS In Refrigerator (35 to 40° F.)	MONTHS In Freezer (0° F.)
Steaks (beef)	3 to 5	8 to 12
Chops (lamb and pork)	3 to 5	3 to 4
Ground Meats	1 to 2	2 to 3
Stew Meats	1 to 2	2 to 3
Roasts (beef and lamb)	3 to 5	8 to 12
Roasts (pork)	3 to 5	4 to 8
Liver and Variety Meats	1 to 2	3 to 4
Corned Brisket	7	½
Frankfurters	7	½
Bacon	7	1
Sausage (pork)	1 to 2	1 to 2
Ham (half)	3 to 5	1 to 2
Ham (slices)	3	1 to 2
Ham (canned)	6 months	Don't freeze
Luncheon Meats	3 to 5	Don't freeze
Sausage (smoked)	7	Don't freeze
Sausage (dry and semidry)	14 to 21	Don't freeze

Reminder: Label and date—not only with the date you put the package *in* but also with the "expiration date," by which time you should check it *out*. Follow the chart on page 226 for an idea of how long specific meats can be stored before quality begins to go noticeably downhill. Note that these times apply *only* if your freezer stays at 0° or colder. If your sole freezer space is over the refrigerator compartment and has no separate door, don't count on keeping foods frozen for longer than a week: A constant temperature of 0° just isn't possible under those conditions.

To thaw: First know that frozen meat can be cooked satisfactorily while still in its frozen state (with the exception of thick pork steaks and pork roasts, which must be at least partially thawed in order to insure thorough cooking). But if you do choose to thaw your meat before cooking, a few easy dos and don'ts will help to keep it in the pink of condition.

Slow-thaw method—If possible, allow meat to thaw, still freezer-wrapped, in the refrigerator. For a 3- to 5-pound roast, it will take 3 to 5 hours per pound. For a 1-inch steak, count on approximately 12 to 14 hours.

Fast-thaw method—Although there is some chance of spoilage, meat *can* be thawed at room temperature. Keep wrapped. For small roasts, allow 1 to 2 hours per pound. For a 1-inch steak, allow 2 to 4 hours. Cook the meat while it's still chilled.

Fastest-thaw method—Meat that is destined to be braised or pot roasted can be thawed by covering the sealed package with cold water. Then there's the . . .

No-thaw method— You can start to cook almost any cut of meat while it's still frozen; just add extra cooking time.

Cooking Frozen Meat

Roasts: A small roast will take from one third to half again as long to cook as one that has been thawed. The actual additional time depends on the thickness. Let the roast cook about an hour before inserting the meat thermometer.

Steaks, chops, burgers: These will take from one fourth to half again as long to cook as meat that has been thawed. To broil—Keep the meat farther away from the heat source than you do when it's thawed; this will prevent it from being charred on the outside and raw in the center. (Add an additional distance of 2 inches for any cut thicker than ¾ inch.) To pan-broil —Be sure to heat the skillet before adding the meat, and brown it quickly. The idea is to beat the thaw to the draw. If the surface starts to thaw *before* it's browned, chances are it won't brown well at all. Once the meat is browned, turn down the heat to let it cook to the desired degree of doneness.

A word about refreezing: Meat, once thawed, can be refrozen *only* if some ice crystals remain. *But* don't expect meat to be as flavorful or juicy if it's refrozen, as some of the good juices will have been lost in the original thaw-out.

FISH

For a change-of-pace, highly nutritious meal that can be as kindly in cost as it is in calories, fish is your dish. What's more, fish is quick to fix, and most varieties come in handy serving-size portions.

Fresh Fish

When you shop for a whole fish, look for bright, clear, bulging eyes; firm flesh that springs back when pressed; reddish-pink gills; shiny, bright-colored scales, close to the skin. All fresh fish should *smell* fresh and not too strong. For each serving, you'll need:

☐ Whole—¾ to 1 pound

☐ Steaks—½ pound ☐ Fillets—⅓ to ½ pound

To store in refrigerator: Wrap in moisture-proof airtight material, or place in a tightly covered container and refrigerate pronto! (Only the coldest section of your refrigerator will do.) If you don't plan to use the fish in a day or two, freeze it.

To freeze: Assuming whole fish has been cleaned (and scaled if necessary), wash under running cold water, drain, gently pat dry and wrap tightly in a moisture-vapor-proof wrap such as heavy foil, freezer paper or plastic wrap.

Steaks and fillets should be separated by a double thickness of foil or waxed paper and then tightly wrapped.

Label and date all packages.

To thaw: Place still-wrapped frozen fish in the refrigerator (allow about 8 hours to thaw a 1-pound package). For speedier thawing, leave fish in its freezer wrap and cover with cold water, changing the water frequently (a 1-pound package will thaw in about 2 hours). Fillets and steaks can be cooked without thawing—but give them extra cooking time.

Frozen Fish

Frozen fish comes in an ever-increasing variety of portions in addition to steaks and fillets—squares, rounds, sticks, rectangles—some breaded, some not, some precooked, some ready for cooking. Aside from relying on the package for directions, there are just a few general "need to knows":

☐ ⅓ to ½ pound serves one.

☐ Fish portions and sticks should go directly from freezer to pan; don't thaw them first. If they do thaw, use immediately; don't refreeze.

☐ Storage limit—6 months.

Shellfish

Although usually considered a luxury, in the small quantities needed for two, shellfish is often no more costly than meat. Especially since it takes so well to being stretched with sauces, pasta or rice. Figure an average serving about like this:

☐ Shrimp—5 to 7 large (about 15 per pound) or 10 to 15 medium (about 28 per pound)

☐ Lobster tails—1 large or 2 small

☐ Lobster meat—¼ pound

☐ Crabmeat—¼ pound

☐ Scallops—⅓ to ½ pound

☐ Oysters, clams—½ pint shucked or 6 in the shell

Be sure the shells of oysters and clams are tightly closed. Shrimp and scallops should have a clean, fresh smell; whole lobsters should be alive (or cooked).

Refrigerate all shellfish promptly and use as soon as possible—within 1 day. Observe the same guidelines for shellfish bought frozen as for other fish.

POULTRY

The pleasures of poultry are many, and not the least of these is economy. But that's just for starters. Count also among its attributes . . .

☐ Variety—dozens of ways to buy it.

☐ Versatility—hundreds of ways to fix it.

☐ Availability—no more just the Sunday chicken and

the Thanksgiving turkey; you can enjoy poultry any day and any season.

How to Buy

Broiler-fryer chicken: About 1½ to 3 pounds; allow ½ to 1 pound per person. Comes fresh or frozen and either ready-to-cook or cooked and ready to reheat. Buy whole, halved, quartered or cut into serving pieces. Also packaged in parts: drumsticks, breasts, thighs, wings, livers, gizzards. Even though you may pay a little more per pound, chicken parts can be a thrifty no-waste buy for two. Besides, you can start with your favorite pieces! The broiler-fryer is really an all-purpose chicken; suitable preparation methods include not only broiling and frying but also roasting and stewing. For casseroles and dishes like creamed chicken, remember that a 2½-pound broiler-fryer yields approximately 2 cups cut-up cooked chicken.

Roaster chicken: Weighing 3½ to 5 pounds, this is a little larger and older than the broiler-fryer. It is the best choice for roasting but can also be used for stewing.

Rock Cornish hen: About 1 to 1½ pounds. The smaller size of this minimember of the chicken family is just right for a single serving; the larger size is fine for two. Usually comes frozen. Can be roasted stuffed or unstuffed, or can be split and broiled.

Duckling: About 3½ to 5 pounds will be fine for two. A special treat for dark-meat lovers, for unlike chicken and turkey, even the breast is dark. Comes whole, fresh or frozen. Roast whole, stuffed or unstuffed, or cut up for braising or baking.

Turkey: A 4- to 9-pound fryer-roaster is the best size for two (allow ½ to 1 pound per person). Comes whole, fresh or frozen; frozen turkeys may be stuffed or unstuffed. Also available halved, quartered, cut into serving pieces or by the part (drumsticks, thighs, wings and occasionally breasts). Roast; cut-up fryer-roaster can also be broiled, panfried, braised or barbecued.

Boneless turkey roll: About 2 to 5 pounds. Comes frozen, with all white meat or a combination of white and dark meat. Available with or without gravy.

Ground turkey: Sold by the pound, like ground meats

(½ pound serves two). Low in fat and low in calories, thrifty, tasty ground turkey is almost as versatile as hamburger. Follow the same storing and freezing directions as for ground beef (see page 226).

How to Store

In the refrigerator: Quick—to the refrigerator . . . and always where it's coldest! Keep loosely covered or in its transparent store wrap. Use within 1 to 2 days.

In the freezer: For short-term storage (up to 2 weeks), the transparent store wrap does nicely for pre-packaged poultry. If you plan to freeze longer, overwrap the store package with a moisture-vapor-proof wrap (heavy-duty foil, plastic wrap or a plastic bag). Or wash, pat dry and wrap snugly in your favorite freezer material. (Giblets should be frozen separately.) And don't forget to label and date packages. Storage limit at 0° or lower:

☐ Poultry—6 months   ☐ Giblets—6 months

To thaw: Slowly, slowly is the best way. Which means thaw in the refrigerator rather than on the kitchen counter. Allow the following times:

☐ Chicken parts—4 to 9 hours
☐ Whole chicken—12 hours
☐ Rock Cornish hen—9 to 12 hours
☐ Turkey parts—9 to 12 hours
☐ 4- to 9-pound turkey—1 to 2 days

In a hurry? Cover frozen poultry, still tightly wrapped, with cold water, changing the water occasionally. A whole chicken will thaw in 1 to 2 hours; a whole turkey in 3 to 4 hours.

Leftover cooked poultry? Store well-wrapped in the refrigerator for 1 to 2 days (*always package any stuffing separately*). Freezer times.

☐ Plain—1 month
☐ With broth or gravy—6 months

Freezing tips: Is poultry frozen beyond the recommended time limits still safe? If properly stored, yes. But don't expect the taste or texture to be as good. Can poultry be refrozen once it's thawed? Better not! Although there is this exception: Frozen, uncooked poultry can be thawed and *cooked* and the leftovers then frozen for another time.

SOME GOOD MEAT CHOICES FOR TWO

LOOK FOR THESE CUTS	COOK THEM PROPERLY
BEEF	
Ground: Use in patties, loaves or main-dish casseroles. Regular (25 to 30% fat, some shrinkage), Lean (20 to 25% fat, less shrinkage), Extra Lean (15 to 20% fat, very little shrinkage).	Broil. Panbroil. Panfry. (Bake loaves and casseroles.)
Short Ribs: Cut from the ends of chuck or rib roasts.	Braise or cook in liquid.
Stew Meat: Cut from chuck, tip, short plate and foreshank. Usually cut into 1-inch pieces; should contain small amount of fat.	Braise or cook in liquid.
Chuck Roast: Choose arm (round bone), blade or boneless roasts; can be cut up and cooked in small quantities.	Braise.
Chuck Steak: Available either boneless or with a round or blade bone. Economical.	Braise. Can be broiled if of high quality or if tenderized.
Top Loin Steak: Small steak in the short loin; has no tenderloin. Just the right size for individual servings.	Broil. (Panbroil if less than 3/4 inch thick.)
Cubed Steak: Also called Minute Steak. Machine-cubed.	Panfry.
Flank Steak: Also called London Broil. Long, coarse fibers; sometimes scored in diamonds for tenderness.	Braise. Can be broiled if of high quality and marinated.
Porterhouse Steak: Has a section of tenderloin and a section of top loin steak divided by a T-shaped bone. Tenderloin can be removed and served separately as Filet Mignon.	Broil. (Panbroil if less than 3/4 inch thick.)
Rib Steak: Cut from the rib section—actually this is a slice of rib roast, with bone or boneless.	Broil. (Panbroil if less than 3/4 inch thick.)

Rib Eye Steak: Also called Delmonico Steak. Cut from the eye of beef rib. Boneless, has little fat, very tender. — Broil. (Panbroil if less than 3/4 inch thick.)

Round Steak: The top round is sometimes more tender than the bottom round. (Large steaks can be cut into meal-size portions.) Economical because of very little waste. — Braise. Can be broiled if of high quality or if tenderized.

Sirloin Steak: Bone in or boneless; the amount of bone varies from steak to steak. Less expensive than most steaks, it's a good choice for two. — Broil. (Panbroil if less than 3/4 inch thick.)

T-Bone Steak: Similar to porterhouse but smaller, with a smaller tenderloin portion. — Broil. (Panbroil if less than 3/4 inch thick.)

Tenderloin Steak: Better known as Filet Mignon. Boneless, very little fat, tenderest of all steaks; expensive. — Broil.

Broiling

For tender steaks and chops, sliced ham, bacon, ground meat, baby beef liver. (Steaks and chops should be at least 3/4 inch thick.)

1. Set oven to broil and/or 550°.
2. Broil with meat surface 2 to 5 inches (depending on thickness) from heat until brown. Season only after browning.
3. Turn and broil to desired degree of doneness. Season.

Panbroiling

For tender steaks and chops, sliced ham, bacon, ground meat. (All cuts should be thin—no more than 1 inch thick.)

1. Place meat in heavy skillet. (For very lean meat cuts, brush skillet with shortening.)
2. Do not add fat or water. Do not cover.
3. Cook slowly. Turn occasionally to brown and cook meat evenly. Pour off fat from skillet as it accumulates.
4. Cook until done. Season.

Panfrying

For thin, tender steaks and chops, cutlets, ground meat, liver and pieces which have been tenderized by scoring, cubing or grinding.

1. Brown on both sides in small amount of fat. (Fat is not needed in a pan with non-stick coating.)
2. Season with salt and pepper.
3. Do not cover.
4. Cook over medium heat, turning occasionally, until done.

SOME GOOD MEAT CHOICES FOR TWO

LOOK FOR THESE CUTS	COOK THEM PROPERLY
PORK	
Bacon: The cured and smoked side of pork.	Broil. Panbroil. Panfry.
Canadian-style Bacon: A cured and smoked boneless loin of pork, leaner than regular bacon.	Roast (bake). Broil. Panbroil. Panfry.
Chops: Blade, rib, loin and sirloin chops are available, cut thick or thin. Extra-thin chops cook quickly and are a time-saver.	Roast (bake). Broil. Panbroil. Braise.
Ham Slice: Cut from smoked ham. Available in a variety of thicknesses.	Roast (bake). Broil. Panbroil. Panfry.
Canned Ham: The 1½-pound size is good for two. Follow directions on can.	Roast (bake).
Ribs: (Spareribs, back ribs and country-style ribs.) Proportion of meat to fat to bone varies considerably; prices vary accordingly.	Roast (bake). Braise.
Sausages: Available in great variety—frankfurters, Polish sausages, bratwurst, knackwurst, etc.	Roast (bake). Broil. Panbroil. Panfry.
Smoked Chops: Only the loin cut is available.	Broil. Roast (bake).
Smoked Shoulder Roll: Boneless. Like Canadian-style bacon, but has more fat distributed throughout the meat. Economical. A 1- to 2-pound size is good for two. Follow package directions or use like ham.	Roast (bake). Cook in liquid. Broil. Panbroil. Panfry.
Steak: Arm or blade cuts are available. A good buy.	Braise. Panfry.
Tenderloin: Boneless; whole, sliced or flattened. Very tender. Frozen tenderloins are good for two; follow package directions.	Roast (bake). Panfry. Braise.

Chops: Shoulder, rib, loin and sirloin chops are available. (Shoulder chops are the most economical.)   Broil. Panbroil.

Ground: Made from the less tender cuts. Shape into meat loaf or patties.   Roast (bake). Broil. Panbroil. Panfry.

Shanks: Foreshanks and hindshanks are available. A 1-pound shank is just right for one person.   Braise. Cook in liquid.

VEAL

Chops: Rib, loin and sirloin chops are available.   Braise. Panfry.

Cutlets: Cut from round steak.   Braise. Panfry.

Roasting

For large, tender cuts of beef, veal, pork and lamb.

1. Place fat side up on rack in shallow roasting pan.
2. Insert meat thermometer so it is centered in thickest part, not resting in fat or on bone.
3. Do not add water. Do not cover.
4. Roast at 325° until done. (See roasting charts for time, temperature and degree of doneness.)

Braising

For less tender meat cuts (pot roasts, round steak, short ribs), stew meat and some tender cuts (pork chops and cutlets).

1. Brown on all sides in heavy pan, skillet or Dutch oven, adding fat if necessary.
2. Season with salt and pepper.
3. Add small amount of liquid if necessary.
4. Cover tightly. Simmer on top of range or in 300 to 325° oven until meat is tender.

Cooking in Liquid

For large, less tender meat cuts (beef corned brisket, pork hocks, lamb shanks) and stew meat.

1. Brown meat on all sides in own fat or other fat, if desired, in heavy pan, skillet or Dutch oven.
2. Cover meat with liquid.
3. Season; cover and simmer until tender.
4. Add vegetables just long enough before serving to cook them through.

SOME GOOD VEGETABLE CHOICES FOR TWO

WHAT TO BUY	WHAT TO LOOK FOR	HOW TO STORE
Artichokes (1 per person)	Thick, green, fresh-looking leaves on plump, compact, globular heads; avoid spreading leaves.	Store in refrigerator, either in crisper or plastic bag. Will keep up to 4 days.
Asparagus (1 bunch—1/2 to 3/4 pound)	Smooth, round spears with a fresh appearance. Tips should be closed and compact.	Store in refrigerator, either in crisper or plastic bag. Will keep up to 2 days.
Cabbage (1 small head—2 cups shredded)	A firm head, with fresh, well-colored outer leaves.	Store in refrigerator, either in crisper or plastic bag. Will keep up to 4 weeks.
Carrots (1 bunch—5 or 6 medium)	Smooth, firm, well shaped; a good orange color.	Store in refrigerator, either in crisper or plastic bag. Will keep up to 2 weeks.
Cauliflower (1 small head or 1/2 large head)	Clean, compact, white to creamy-white curds (the edible white portion); good green leaves.	Store in refrigerator, either in crisper or plastic bag. Will keep up to 5 days.
Celery (1 small bunch)	Crisp, solid stalks with a glossy surface. Avoid bunches with discoloration of center stalks.	Store in refrigerator, either in crisper or plastic bag. Will keep up to 8 days.

Corn on the Cob
(About 4 ears)

Green, fresh-looking husks. The silk at the husk opening should be dark brown, and the ears should be well covered with plump kernels.

For best eating quality, cook as soon as possible after picking. If you must store corn, refrigerate unhusked and uncovered. Will keep up to 2 days.

Cucumber
(1 medium)

Firm, good green color, not too large in diameter. Avoid cucumbers that look withered or shriveled.

Store in refrigerator, either in crisper or plastic bag. Will keep up to 2 weeks.

Eggplant
(1 small—1/2 to 3/4 pound)

Firm, heavy, with smooth skin of an even dark purple color. Avoid eggplants that are soft, shriveled or marked with dark brown spots.

Store in refrigerator, in crisper. Will keep up to 2 weeks.

Lettuce
(1 medium head lettuce yields about 6 cups bite-size pieces)

Fresh, unwilted greens. Head lettuce should be medium firm and of medium size; outer leaves, varying from light to dark green, should be free of rust marks.

Select well-rounded heads of Boston, heavy for their size, with tender leaves ranging from white to medium green.

Look for fairly compact heads of romaine; the long green outer leaves should be stiff, with white to light green ribs.

Store as soon as possible in refrigerator, either in crisper or plastic bag. Before storing, wash lettuce under running cold water; drain or pat dry *thoroughly*. Head and romaine lettuce can be kept up to 1 week, other varieties for a shorter time.

Mushrooms
(1/4 to 1/2 pound)

Firm caps of white or creamy color, depending on the species. Avoid mushrooms with flat, open caps or cracked stems.

Store in refrigerator (spread on shallow pan or tray; cover with damp cloth). Will keep up to 4 days. Before using, wipe with damp cloth or rinse and wipe dry.

SOME GOOD VEGETABLE CHOICES FOR TWO

WHAT TO BUY	WHAT TO LOOK FOR	HOW TO STORE
Onions (½ pound)	Hard, firm globes; paper-thin outer skins. (Yellow and white globe onions are the most common and are primarily used for cooking. Bermuda-type onions have a mild flavor and are ideal for slicing, eating [raw] and cooking. Spanish onions are easy to slice and great in salads.)	Store in a cool, dry, well ventilated place. Onions will keep for 2 weeks at room temperature, longer at a temperature of 45 to 50°. Do not refrigerate.
Parsley (1 bunch)	Crisp, bright, deep green leaves.	Store in refrigerator. Before storing, wash under running cold water, then shake to remove excess moisture. Place in jar and cover.
Peppers (Sweet Bell) (1 medium)	Relatively heavy in weight, with firm, well-shaped, thick "walls." Color should be a medium to dark green.	Store in refrigerator, either in crisper or plastic bag. Will keep up to 5 days.
Potatoes (2 medium potatoes or ¾ pound new potatoes)	Evenly shaped, mature, of medium size, firm and without cuts, blemishes, green discoloration or sprouts. General-purpose potatoes—like Russet Burbank, Cherokee, Kennebec—are mealy and excellent for baking and mashing. New potatoes should be well shaped, firm, free from blemishes and sunburn; they are ideal boiled and in salads.	Store at room temperature, in a place with good ventilation. Will keep up to 2 weeks—longer at 45 to 50° temperature. Do not refrigerate. New potatoes will keep up to 4 days—longer at 45 to 50° temperature.

Spinach (1 pound of fresh spinach, cooked)	Crisp, dark green leaves; avoid leaves that are crushed or wilted.	Store in refrigerator. Will keep up to 3 days. Before using, remove imperfect leaves and root ends. Wash just before using if spinach is to be cooked. For salads, wash leaves, drain and dry.
Squash (1 medium acorn squash or 2 to 4 zucchini)	Tough-skinned acorn squash, hard and heavy for its size; avoid sunken or moldy spots and skin punctures. Zucchini should be firm and well formed with tender, glossy skins.	*Acorn squash:* Store at room temperature; will keep up to 2 weeks—longer at 60° temperature. Do not refrigerate. *Zucchini:* Store in refrigerator, either in crisper or plastic bag. Will keep up to 5 days.
Sweet Potatoes (2 medium)	Smooth, plump, dry; uniform in shape and color.	Store at room temperature, with good ventilation. Will keep up to 2 weeks—longer at 60° temperature. Do not refrigerate.
Tomatoes (1 pound)	Well formed, smooth, well ripened and reasonably free of blemishes.	Store in refrigerator, in crisper. Will keep up to 1 week. (If necessary, keep at room temperature until ripe.)

SOME GOOD FRUIT CHOICES FOR TWO

WHAT TO BUY	WHAT TO LOOK FOR	HOW TO STORE
Apples (about 3 medium in 1 pound)	Firm, crisp, with good color. Avoid apples that are bruised or have a shriveled appearance. For eating, Delicious, McIntosh, Winesap and Northern Spy are among the best. For cooking, Baldwin, Greening and Winesap are good choices.	Store in a cool, dry place or in refrigerator. Will keep up to 2 weeks.
Avocados (1 is enough for 2 servings)	Slightly soft—it should yield to gentle pressure. Avoid avocados with sunken spots or broken surfaces.	Store at room temperature until soft to the touch. When ripe, place in warmest section of refrigerator. Will keep up to 5 days.
Bananas (about 3 medium in 1 pound)	Firm fruit, fully ripened or green. A ripened banana should have a uniform yellow color and brown specks.	Store at room temperature until ripe—bananas ripen quickly. Never refrigerate unless fully ripened.
Cantaloupe (½ to 1 medium per person)	Skin of yellowish-gray or pale yellow color, with a texture like coarse, thick netting. Should have a pleasant cantaloupe odor.	Store in refrigerator in a plastic bag—the bag helps to confine the odor. Will keep up to 8 days. (If necessary, keep at room temperature until ripe.)
Grapefruit (1 is enough for 2 servings)	Firm, smoothly textured, well shaped, heavy for its size. Thin-skinned grapefruit are very juicy. Avoid grapefruit with pointed stem ends or rough, wrinkled skins.	Store in refrigerator or in a cool place. Will keep 2 weeks or longer.

Item	Selection	Storage
Grapes (½ to 1 pound)	Well colored, plump; firmly attached to the stem.	Store unwashed and uncovered in refrigerator. Will keep up to 5 days.
Oranges (2 to 3 oranges yield 1 cup of juice)	Firm, heavy for their size. Navel oranges (seedless) are best for slices and sections; Valencia oranges are preferred for juice.	Store uncovered in refrigerator or in a cool place. Will keep 2 weeks or longer.
Peaches (about 3 medium in 1 pound)	Fairly firm or just a trifle soft. The skin color between the red areas should be yellow or creamy.	Store in refrigerator, in crisper. Will keep up to 1 week. (If necessary, keep at room temperature until ripe.)
Pears (about 3 medium in 1 pound)	For Bartletts, look for a pale yellow to rich yellow color; for D'Anjou or Comice, light green to yellowish green; for Bosc, greenish yellow to brownish yellow. All varieties should be firm.	Store in refrigerator, in crisper. (If necessary, keep at room temperature until ripe.)
Pineapple (1 is enough for 2 servings)	Heavy for its size, slightly soft, golden in color. The fruit should have a fragrant pineapple odor. Avoid fruit with signs of decay at the base or on sides.	Store in refrigerator or in a cool place. Will keep up to 2 days. Wrap the pineapple in a plastic bag—the bag helps to keep the fragrance confined to the pineapple.
Strawberries (1 pint)	Firm berries of a bright, lustrous color; caps and stems should be firmly attached.	Store unwashed and uncovered in refrigerator. Will keep up to 2 days.

HOW MUCH IS ENOUGH?

FOOD	IF YOU HAVE...	YOU'LL GET...
Apple	1 medium	1 cup chopped
Banana	1 to 2 medium	1 cup sliced
	3 medium	1 cup mashed
Beans, dried (small)	8 ounces	3 cups cooked
Butter or margarine	1 pound	2 cups
	¼ pound or 1 stick	½ cup
Cabbage	¼ pound	1 cup shredded
Carrots	1 to 2 medium	1 cup shredded
	2 to 3 medium	1 cup thinly sliced
Celery	2 medium stalks	1 cup sliced
Cereal (flakes)	3 cups	1 cup crushed
Cheese		
Cheddar or American	4 ounces	1 cup shredded
cottage	8 ounces	1 cup
cream	3-ounce package	6 tablespoons
	8-ounce package	1 cup (16 tbs.)
Chicken (cooked)	2½-pound broiler-fryer	2 cups diced
Chocolate		
chips	6-ounce package	1 cup
unsweetened	8-ounce package	8 squares (1 oz. each)
Crackers		
graham	12 squares	1 cup fine crumbs
soda	20 squares	1 cup coarse crumbs
Cream		
sour	8 ounces	1 cup
whipping	1 cup (½ pint)	2 cups whipped
Flour		
all-purpose	1 pound	3½ cups
cake	1 pound	4 cups
Green pepper	1 medium	1 cup chopped
Lemon		
juice	1 medium	2 to 3 tablespoons
peel	1 medium	1½ teaspoons grated
Macaroni (elbow)	½ of 8-ounce pkg.	2 cups cooked
Meat (cooked)	6 to 7 ounces	1 cup julienne strips
Milk (evaporated)	1 can (6 ounces)	⅔ cup
	1 can (14½ ounces)	1⅔ cups
Noodles (regular)	4 ounces	2 cups cooked
Nuts	4 ounces (shelled)	1 cup chopped
Onions	1 medium	½ cup chopped
Rice		
brown	½ cup (uncooked)	1¾ to 2 cups cooked
parboiled (converted)	½ cup (uncooked)	1½ to 1¾ cups cooked
precooked (instant)	1 cup (uncooked)	1 to 2 cups cooked
regular white	½ cup (uncooked)	1½ cups cooked
wild	½ cup (uncooked)	1½ cups cooked
Strawberries	1 pint	2 cups sliced
Sugar		
brown (firmly packed)	1 pound	2¼ cups
confectioners' (unsifted)	1 pound	4 cups
granulated	1 pound	2¼ cups